Famous Artists

AND

THEIR MODELS

AS FOR ME, GIVE ME A BOOK!

BOB AND CAROL

Famous Artists
AND
THEIR MODELS

by

Thomas Craven

POCKET BOOKS, Inc., New York

Famous Artists

AND

THEIR MODELS

POCKET BOOK edition published May, 1949
1st printing...April, 1949
2nd printing...June, 1949

DESIGNED BY MAXWELL MARXE

Notice — *Pocket Book* editions are published only by POCKET BOOKS, INC. and POCKET BOOKS OF CANADA, LTD. Trade-mark Registered in the United States Patent Office

The text of this *Pocket Book* is printed from brand-new plates made from newly set, large, clear, easy-to-read type. The illustrations are printed from new engraved cylinders made specially for this edition.

H

PRINTED IN THE U.S.A.

Contents

Contents

List of Illustrations

THERE is an old saying that one man's dish is another man's poison, an observation, I have perceived, that applies with particular force to painters and their models. One artist, Rubens, for example, prefers nudes; another, like Cézanne, is neurasthenically afraid of women and at home only in the vegetable kingdom; a third, Turner, loves the sea; a fourth, Delacroix, the fury of battle—et cetera. Why this should be so is something for the future of psychology, but the fact remains that artists, like everybody else, are creatures of temperament and individual preferences. A happy condition indeed; for it lends infinite variety to pictures, and one of the many glories of art is that we have enough for every conceivable kind of taste, and enough quantitatively to fill the huge stockpiles known as museums.

During recent years, you have heard many times from the camps of certain artists the prolonged cry that it makes no difference what the subject may be—the important thing is how one paints it. This sort of reasoning has led to some of the most farfetched and meaningless pictures of modern times, and carried to its logical conclusion, as it has been carried by several denominations of artists, it has eliminated the subject entirely, leaving only a residue in the shape of a diagram, or pattern, or abstraction. You are welcome to that form of art, if you like it. To me it is like a wine cask without the wine, and I prefer paintings that depict, and dramatize, and illuminate subjects which we may encounter and appreciate in our daily experiences in the world.

It needs to be said again that the art business has two sides to it: first, the subject, and second, the way in which the subject is treated. One without the other is only half the battle, but the two together, in proper proportion, transform the raw material of nature into the finished product, the work of art. It makes no difference to one artist what models his competitor may choose, but it makes all the difference in the world that he himself, as a creative personality, should choose subjects for which he has strong emotional predilections. The late Grant Wood, working in the corn belt of Iowa, his native state, founded a movement which, for want of a better name, was called regionalism. The movement eventually got out of bounds and Wood repudiated it. He meant by regionalism, not that one subject was intrinsically better than another, or that the material afforded by the Middle West was more significant than that of North Carolina or New York; he meant only to emphasize the old truth that the artist must be rooted to some strong native tendencies in order to make the most of his talents.

Happy is the artist who has a natural and unforced interest in his subjects, who discovers in good season what is uniquely his dish and sticks to it until he has transformed it into a work of art. In truth, it might be said that unless an artist has a special interest in certain subjects and models he is not an artist; and he is a benighted fellow, for sure, if he cannot find in the whole wide world some subject that he can call his own—something that becomes associated with his name.

But once an artist of stature has made a name for himself by painting certain models, a host of nondescripts comes along in his wake, imitating not only his style and personality but also his subjects. When Charles Burchfield made haunting works of art out of ramshackle country stores and dilapidated houses, a veritable school of little Burchfields arose and copied his subjects in the vain hope of lifting themselves into notice. Thomas Benton, by following his natural inclinations, created a legion of hillbilly painters; and Picasso, by concocting neoclassical faces, is responsible for thousands of phony Grecian heads.

How the painter uses his subject matter, the second part of the art business, depends wholly upon his personality. Without personality, he would be no better than a machine, and without an integrated personality, he would be a wild man. His peculiar talents must be disciplined and conditioned by the hardest kind of training and by the range of his experiences. If he is a Van Gogh, poorly trained and emotionally unbalanced, his art will be a molten eruption; if he is bound to the routine of the academies, his pictures will be hard and tight, like those of David and Ingres; if he is capable of preserving his massive personality after years of concentrated study, he may develop into a Rubens who could bend his brush to almost anything. And Rubens, as Aldous Huxley pointed out, was no maker of patterns and abstractions. He loved the nude and made it the symbol of the opulence and splendor he demanded of life. He had the sentiment, not of the abstract hemisphere, but of the breast and the buttock.

You are under no compulsion to like all the paintings reproduced in the following pages; for you will respond only to those in which you can participate, which contain at least a part of yourself. I have brought together a representative group of painters, and have told, in the brief space allotted to each, what they painted and how you would expect them to paint, after a little insight into their lives, habits, and personalities. To simplify matters, I have made the word model all-inclusive, a term to define the artist's subject, whether it be a landscape, a ship, a bird, or a human being.   THOMAS CRAVEN

IN HIS fifty-second year, Leonardo recorded the following item in his notebook:

"On July 6, 1504, Wednesday, at seven in the morning, died Ser Piero da Vinci, notary to the Palazzo del Podesta, my father. He was eighty years of age and left ten sons and two daughters."

That was all. It is not written that the son referred to his sire again, for the finest intelligence that ever found its way into the art of painting was, in part, scientific and curiously devoid of conventional sentiments. As an artist, Leonardo was intimate and tender, but as a scientist, he was detached and solitary, a genius who walked alone far ahead of his contemporaries. There is perhaps another reason for his reticence about his father. He was an illegitimate child, his mother being a peasant girl of sixteen who surrendered her son, for a consideration, and became the wife of a craftsman.

The boy had no remembrance of his youthful mother, but it is known that from her he inherited his personal charm, his strong, slender hands and his golden hair. By the grace of his father, he was endowed with a powerful frame, good health and a zest for life—the old lawyer was married four times and his youngest child appeared fifty years after the first-born, Leonardo.

After a childhood spent in the mountains near the village of Vinci, Leonardo was received at his father's house in Florence. Though no particular stigma was attached to illegitimacy in those days, his half brothers and sisters called him the kitchen wench's bastard and seized upon his irregular birth as an excuse to get rid of him. They were jealous of the boy, for he was miraculously gifted and plainly destined to the highest eminence in those fields where mind and imagination were concerned.

The precocious Leonardo displayed his capacities in many directions—in mathematics, music and every branch of design—improvising words and harmonies for the lute, modeling figures in relief, and drawing animals at play, human faces and flowers. At thirteen, after the custom of the time, he was apprenticed to a master: to Verrocchio, a great sculptor, an admirable painter and a scholar of wide culture. The world of Florence lay before him, the resplendent Tuscan city at the height of its power and grandeur under the most civilized scoundrel of the Renaissance, Lorenzo the Magnificent. He remained with Verrocchio for twelve years, living soberly at the master's house, his fame rising, and by common consent the most lavishly gifted and enviable young man in Italy.

During his apprenticeship and his first years as an independent artist, Leonardo's mind was incessantly active. Continually experimenting, not only with the phenomena of the arts but also in every subdivision of science, he acquired a fabulous and somewhat sinister reputation. In painting, he employed his intellect profoundly, resolving the various problems, both spiritual and technical; and as the first modern man of science, he observed organic life minutely and tested his theories by the laboratory method. He strove to bring about the conjunction of art and science, hoping ultimately to create spontaneously like God himself. From his first period in Florence only three pictures survive: the *St. Jerome* in the Vatican, the *Adoration of the Magi* in the Uffizi, and the *Virgin of the Rocks* in the Louvre, none of them materially profitable and two unfinished. In these years, however, he lived fastidiously and well, keeping servants and a stable of horses, and the conclusion is that he was far more productive than extant paintings would indicate.

Leonardo did not find Florence congenial, despite the reputation of the city as the planetary center of art and culture. "The place is festering with pawnbrokers, tanners, bankers, and conspirators," he wrote in his notebook, "and much too provincial for me." Accordingly, in his thirtieth year, he entered the service of the Duke of Milan, having specified his qualifications in a letter that remains a masterpiece of objective self-analysis. He recommended himself as a military, civil and sanitary engineer, an inventor of all sorts of ballistic and fearsome engines of warfare, and finally, as a painter and sculptor second to none.

The letter is truly an amazing document, and coming from another, Benvenuto Cellini, for instance, we should be inclined to dismiss it as a piece of egregious bragging. In part, he wrote:

"I have a method of constructing very light and portable bridges, to be used in pursuit of, or in retreat from, the enemy, with others of a stronger sort, proof against fire, and easy to fix or remove.

"I have also most convenient and portable bombs, proper for throwing showers of small missiles, and with the smoke thereof causing great terror to the enemy.

"I can also construct covered wagons, secure and indestructible, which, entering among the enemy, will break the strongest bodies of men; and behind these the infantry will follow in safety and without impediment.

"I can make mortars and fieldpieces of beautiful and useful shape, entirely different from those in common use.

"In time of peace, I believe that I could equal any other as regards works in architecture. I can prepare designs for buildings, whether public or private, and also conduct water from one place to another.

"Furthermore, I can execute works in sculpture —marble, bronze, or terra cotta. In painting also I can do what may be done, as well as any other, whosoever he may be.

"And if any of the above-named things shall seem to any man impossible or impracticable, I am perfectly ready to make trial of them in whatever place you shall be pleased to command, commending myself to you with all possible humility."

In Milan, Leonardo lived unostentatiously, with his pupils and assistants, painted the Duke's mistresses, organized festivals, and supplied the court with an artistic background. His sojourn in northern Italy is memorable for his intermittent labors on a gigantic equestrian statue that was never cast; the formulation of his *Notebooks*, one of the indubitably great repositories of the human spirit in its loftiest manifestations; and the execution of *The Last Supper*, the most famous picture in the world. When the French crossed the Alps and imprisoned his patron, the Duke, Leonardo moved on: first, to enter the employ of Cesare Borgia as a military engineer; and second, to return to Florence to fulfill an old painting contract with the city fathers. In Florence, he designed and perfected the portrait of *Mona Lisa;* and having grown weary of the town, traveled to Rome, only to be snubbed by Raphael and his fat protector, Leo X.

At the end of two wasted years in the Eternal City, he journeyed northward to France, invited there by Francis I, an ardent admirer. Appropriately lodged in a château, in Touraine, he was, at last, at peace with the world, and one day, in his precise left-handed script, he wrote in his notebook: "When I thought I had been learning how to live, I had only been learning how to die." Calmly, he offered his soul to God and the Virgin, and at his death, in his sixty-seventh year, a long succession of Masses was celebrated for the comfort of his extraordinary soul.

Leonardo was a lordly figure, and you may search the annals of art from beginning to end without finding another painter who so completely dominated his materials. He was the commander of his subjects: nothing in the human family, or in external nature, disturbed his self-control or made him the slave of his passions; and he ruled over his subjects with the celestial composure of the architect of all creation. Striving consciously for universality, he came closer to his goal than any other man, and the scope of his powers was all-inclusive. No woman ever deranged or seduced him, and when the distaffs, humble or proud, sat to him, he portrayed them as emblems of divine beauty, as in the *Virgin of the Rocks*, or as the psychophysical enigmas embodied in *Mona Lisa* and the sensual *Leda*.

With perfection uppermost in his mind, he worked slowly and with infinite pains, and as a consequence, produced fewer paintings than any other artist of the first rank. His drawings, however, are not only exceedingly abundant but the most flawless examples of their kind the world has enjoyed. "All that is beautiful," he said, "even humanly beautiful, dies—save in art," and his drawings bear out the contention. Thousands upon thousands of his graphic works exist in various collections: some in pastel, a medium he invented; some in silver-point and red chalk, and the greater number in simple pen and ink, the strokes running slantwise from left to right, unmistakable evidence of the southpaw artist.

He made drawings of animals—wolves, dogs, cats and bears—and synthetic creatures such as dragons and unicorns to satisfy his love of the fantastic; but more often than not, he delineated horses, his own magnificent stallions rearing and charging, dramatic horses drawn by a searching student of anatomy and humanized as no quadrupeds have been before or since. He contrived allegories and masquerades for his princely patron, and rendered in caricature, to appease his own curiosity, the faces of grotesque and eccentric characters, with amazing topographical maps thrown in for good measure. In anatomy, he had no peer except perhaps his irascible junior and compatriot, Michelangelo. He dissected some thirty cadavers, and was the first to draw the human embryo in the uterus; and his studies of skulls, nerves and muscles are the last word in precision draftsmanship. But no matter how accurate his observation, the artist in him inevitably triumphed; and his design of the interior of a woman's torso, or of the structure of the beating heart, each graced and modeled into soft, smoky organizations, are, as he asserted, as beautiful in their own way as his drawings of Madonnas, or innocent children frolicking with kittens.

Besides his studies of the nude, for which he utilized the corpses of the morgue and by solicitation, the nakedness of courtesans, he executed, at twenty-one, the first independent landscape in Occidental art, a drawing of the valley of the Arno, which was followed, in after years, by turbulent cloud formations as abstract as the patterns of a twentieth-century cubist. His floral pictures are little masterpieces; and apart from his renderings of nature, he constructed plans for buildings and entire cities with sanitation facilities, as well as instruments of warfare nearly five hundred years before his time—airplanes propelled by spring motors, tanks of modern design and military engines of effectual and devilish contrivance.

Preoccupied with an ideal of absolute perfection, Leonardo left only a few paintings—haunting, baffling works in which body and soul were consummately blended by an artist sternly disciplined in both. He created a type of smiling woman after the example of the archaic Greeks, avowing that the Almighty God would plant a smile on the face of the perfect woman, once He had fashioned her. While he was making the preliminary drawings for *The Last Supper*, he stopped momentarily to invent a machine for grinding sausage meat; and the fundamental brainwork expended on the greatest single picture in the world would have killed the average artist. He roamed the Milanese ghetto, notebook in hand, for expressive faces, observed condemned men about to be hanged for his drawing of Judas, and after two years of searching, found a suitable model for Christ in a princely Jewish youth. *The Last Supper*, now, alas blurred and faded! was the first to exhibit the psychological effects of dramatic action—the impact on the apostles of the pronouncement, "One of you shall betray Me!"

Kings and princesses vied with one another to enlist the services of Leonardo, but with scant success. In the line of duty he depicted the charms of Cecilia and Lucrezia, the favored mistresses of his employer, the Duke of Milan; but when the Duke's sister-in-law, Isabella d'Este, a truly remarkable woman of gentle breeding and catholic tastes in the arts, sought to attach him to her court at Mantua and to relieve her infatuation in a fashion something less than platonic, she was rebuffed with dignity and indifference. Leonardo was heedless of her pleas for "a little twelve-year-old Christ, or a little Madonna, devout and sweet," but he did tarry long enough at her palace to take a likeness of her in red chalk.

Only twice, so far as the records go, did the master expend all his powers on the portrayal of women: once in a painting of the ancient myth of *Leda and the Swan*, a picture no longer extant, but to judge by the copies, an incomparable conception of soft and insinuating desire; and again in *Mona Lisa*, the lady with the glance, as Gautier put it, "which, though divinely ironical, promises endless voluptuousness."

The *Mona Lisa* is probably the most perfect picture of the western world; the face, despite the fading of the flesh tones, being the subtlest piece of modeling ever done, and the hands, beyond dispute, the most beautiful in art. The sitter was Madame Lisa, third wife of Francesco del Giocondo, and according to all accounts, exceedingly alluring. The husband was an expert on Swiss cattle and raw sheepskins, and the wife, a sensitive soul, came alone to the studio of Leonardo to be painted.

The figure of the woman is as solid and permanently established as the rocks behind it, for the artist believed that solidity is one of the cardinal prerequisites of the art of painting. Yet the figure is free to bend and breathe and move, and is brought into the highest relief by the purposely strange background of dwindling rivers and shadowy peaks—by a landscape wrought out with as much affection as the smiling face.

The face of the woman, I need hardly say, is the most discussed face in the world's great portrait gallery, and the smile has been the subject of endless speculations, some mysterious and uncanny, some meaningless and Freudian. Technically, the smile was achieved by imperceptible variations in the lines of the eyes and mouth, and by modeling of the utmost delicacy.

The smile is not peculiar to Mona Lisa, nor was it original with Leonardo. You will find a similar baffling expression on the faces of the archaic goddesses of Greece, and in the sculptures of his master Verrocchio, and in other paintings of the time. Every artist, especially where the human face is concerned, seems unconsciously to favor a certain expressive mood, and to create his own type of face to embody that mood, or state of the soul, as Michelangelo put it. Leonardo, for his own private reasons, loved to portray the smile and used it to give life and reality and the illusion of spiritual depth to his characters. The mysteries attached to Mona Lisa arose from the romantic gossip surrounding the model and to the misconceptions of the artist's purpose. According to the old fables, the model was a strange and uncanny charmer, a sphinx whose smile entrapped the soul of a great artist and impelled him to build up, bit by bit, an image of impenetrable mystery. The truth is, I fear, that he had no romantic interest in the model and that he found her smile artistically useful.

The artist worked at the portrait intermittently for three years, and in order to induce the proper mood in Mona Lisa, posed her only in the twilight hours in a background of irises and lilies, her favorite flowers, with fountains playing and musicians performing to exalt her spirit. But with the almost unattainable standard of perfection which characterized all his work, Leonardo declared the portrait unfinished, refused to part with it, and carried it off to France where eventually it fell into the hands of the king, his last patron. The woman upon whom he had bestowed the fulness of his genius failed to influence him, and when he departed this life, he left behind him not only the legendary fame usually associated with necromancers and magicians, but a most substantial body of evidence in support of the old saying that a great artist is the master of his models.

Right: Plate 1

LEONARDO DA VINCI

Head of Christ

Plate 2

LEONARDO DA VINCI
Mary, Jesus, St. Elizabeth and St. John

Plate 3

LEONARDO DA VINCI
Mary, Jesus and St. Anne

Plate 4

MICHELANGELO
Adam
·(DETAIL FROM *The Creation*)

Plate 5

MICHELANGELO
Jeremiah

Plate 6

TITIAN
Toilet of Venus

Plate 7

TITIAN
The Man with the Glove

.X°. IVLII. ANNO.
.H. VIII. XXVIII°.
ETATIS SVÆ
ANNO XXXIII

Plate 8

HOLBEIN

Portrait of Richard Southwell

WALT WHITMAN once referred to Abraham Lincoln as the Michelangelo of the West, a shrewd observation if the metaphor is not pushed too far. The similarity is not physical, although both were homely enough according to classical standards, Lincoln being tall and lean and noble, the Florentine artist short, shriveled and irascible, with a nose broken in his student days by a jealous rival. The resemblance lay in the spiritual depth of the two men: the profound convictions, the unparalleled humanity and the pursuit of the loftiest ideals in the face of obstacles that would have killed anyone of smaller stature.

Like the American, Michelangelo was born of broken-down stock on his father's side, but unlike Lincoln he was spared the assassin's bullet and lived to be nearly ninety years old, productive to the last breath. His patrons were the popes and he slaved for nine of them; he saw the glory of the Renaissance fade into hypocritical culture and Italy ruined by butchers from the North; and he saw the city of Florence, "the very air of which," he asseverated, "was conducive to the birth of divine genius," sold down the Arno by native sons. He was endowed with indomitable resolution, the will to conceive and execute stupendous works of art, and in sculpture so powerful and comprehensive were his achievements—and they were only a fraction of his ambitions—as to exhaust the art of carving which, since his time, has drifted along without direction or purpose.

At school in Florence, Michelangelo exhibited prodigious ability in drawing, and in his thirteenth year was accepted by Ghirlandaio, the most popular artist in the town, as a qualified assistant on a small retainer. Insultingly critical of his associates because their goal was short of absolute perfection, he dominated his master's workshop, and it is not likely that he learned much from Ghirlandaio except the technique of fresco painting, the application of water color to wet plaster. By a stroke of good luck, the relationship was terminated in a year by Lorenzo the Magnificent, who took the boy under his wing to make a sculptor out of him. Lorenzo treated his protégé as one of his own sons, seating him at table in the company of the finest intellects of Italy, giving him a liberal stipend and a studio to work in, and best of all, allowing him to develop his genius for sculpture in the Medicean gardens surrounded by examples of Hellenic carvings or replicas by proud Romans. "It was only well with me," he confessed in his last years, "when I had a mallet and chisel in my hands," and painting, he avowed, particularly easel-painting, "was an occupation fit for women and mules." In addition to his training at Lorenzo's villa, he pursued his studies of anatomy by night in his own room; and having pleased the prior of one of the churches by a crucifix carved in wood, he was rewarded by a nook in which he secreted and dissected dead bodies. These ghoulish enterprises turned his stomach permanently and henceforth he was not able to eat or drink with relish.

At eighteen, on the strength of two carvings, one a *Madonna and Child*, the other a pagan piece, *The Battle of the Centaurs*, he stood alone in his profession, above and apart from the conniving ruck; and at twenty-one, went to Rome to seek his fortune. His attainments in paint and marble remain one of the authentic wonders of the world, and his material returns, in houses, estates, and hoarded cash, were comparable to those of the pawnbrokers and titled politicians—yet he had no use for money and lived meanly, sleeping in his clothes, eating little, and denying himself the relaxing pleasures of the average successful man.

At twenty-five he carved the *Pietà*, now in a chapel of St. Peter's, and for the city of Florence, the *Giant*, or *David*, out of an eighteen-foot slab abandoned as intractable by other sculptors. Goaded and bullied by Julius II, a gruff and formidable soul like himself, he projected a colossal tomb for the Pontiff, only three statues of which were completed; and after a terrific argument, surrendered to the supreme Vicar and decorated the ceiling of the Sistine Chapel.

In Florence during the sack of Rome by Charles V, he constructed the fortresses of the city, between times, chiseling in stone ambidextrously the statues of the Medici Sacristy. Back in the Eternal City, he was called in by Paul III as chief architect, painter and sculptor at the Vatican, and in his triple capacity, executed *The Last Judgment* behind the high altar of the Sistine Chapel; hacked out, in his old age, a *Descent from the Cross* which makes tombstones out of most sculpture; and drafted the dome for the remodeled St. Peter's. In 1564, he was at work on a plan for a great Crucifixion in marble, when a slow fever attacked and consumed him.

It is impossible to measure the attainments of Michelangelo by the standards governing the efforts of ordinary artists. He created a world inhabited by a race of supermen—not simply muscular giants actuated by brute strength, but an heroic breed of men and women capable in mind and body alike of reshaping the universe on an omnipotent scale. There is nothing small in his world, nothing mean or picayune or precious or ornamental—only colossal forms in a background of unmitigated bleakness. Thus, in his handiwork on the ceiling of the Sistine Chapel—an architectonic scheme supporting massive figures whose various actions symbolize the creation of the Mosaic world, man's first disobedience, and the prophecies of redemption—landscape is stripped to its barest essentials, the vegetable kingdom indicated by a handful of herbs, and Paradise by a stretch of barren ground relieved by some rocks and one tree!

Michelangelo was not blind to the physical beauty of youths and maidens, and in his only easel-painting, *The Holy Family* of the Uffizi Gallery, the Virgin Mother was drawn from a magnificent peasant model, a *contadina* in the full bloom of womanhood; while the young lady who posed for the divine Mother in the *Pietà* of St. Peter's, according to the testimony of the artist, was physically and spiritually a virgin. When the carpers of his own day objected to the youthfulness of the Mother, Michelangelo retorted: "Don't you know that chaste women retain their freshness far longer than the unchaste? How much more would this be the case of a virgin into whose heart there has never crept a lascivious desire! Nay, I will go farther and hazard the belief that such unsullied bloom of youth may have been miraculously wrought to convince the world of the virginity and perpetual purity of the Mother."

It was his practice to generalize the human face into an ideal countenance emphasizing purity or power, and for the most part he left portraiture to other hands. Under duress, he made a likeness of Pope Julius in bronze, a huge affair rising above fourteen feet in a sitting posture, only to have his labors annulled by the doughty Pope's enemies. The bronze was melted down and cast into a cannon, and the head, which weighed six hundred pounds, was spirited away never to be recovered. Ordered to carve the portrait statues of a couple of obscure Medicean dukes in the Sacristy at Florence, he complied by idealizing their faces into serene and exalted reflections of human dignity. "In one hundred years," he said, "no one will know or care who they were."

At the age of sixty-three he met Vittoria Colonna, a childless widow of noble birth, far from glamorous, with a sharp angular face not likely to attract connoisseurs of beauty. Her charms were spiritual; she was, in fact, the only woman Michelangelo condescended to visit, and her affection, he said, "kept his old heart, so near the point of death, alive." In a convent near Rome, on Sunday mornings, he went to see her, and on one occasion, she sat for a portrait drawing, an elaborately finished study that should serve as a model and a warning to practitioners of the formless, modernist style.

Male or female, the sexual attributes of his models were unemphasized and unimportant. An eighteen-foot distaff cannot be equipped with sex appeal; that is, for anyone less than a male giant, and had Michelangelo given his women the voluptuous blandishments of the Venetian school, his oversize nudes would be monstrous and revolting. His incomparable reclining figures in the Medici Sacristy at Florence were carved from large women who had labored under many pregnancies, and they symbolize eternal compassion, if not shame, for the sons of men. No other statues of nakedness can be mentioned in the same breath with them, but they are fundamentally sexless. His *Giant*, or *David*, in Florence, was hewn from an adolescent model whose body was proportionately adapted to the requirements of a long, flat, slab, and in his extreme old age, he chiseled a portrait of himself as one of the supporters of Christ.

Only once did Michelangelo incorporate a purely sexual element into his art. Pestered by the agent of the Duke of Ferrara for a sample of his genius, he fell back on the ancient theme cherished by Renaissance collectors—the myth of Leda and the Swan. The results transcended nature, but did little credit to the emaciated Florentine. The artist depicted a situation not usually reserved for painters: an act of coition as it had never been visualized before, a tremendous fornication between a female of Herculean vigor and no glamor, and a swan of savage impulsions. Disgusted with the whole performance, Michelangelo refused to part with the painting and presented it to one of his servants. It survives today only in copies—some of them obscenely retouched. It was no disaster and it only proves that Michelangelo, when he essayed to be sexual, was only frightening.

The murals on the ceiling of the Sistine Chapel, done by this shrunken Florentine lying flat on a scaffold, constitute the greatest singlehanded work of art thus far produced by the world of men. The decorations number some 343 figures, 225 of which range from ten to eighteen feet in height, with children interspersed, little six-footers, to round out the big family. The figures include nude athletes bursting with vitality, the Delphic Sibyl, the noblest superwoman ever conceived, the terrifying Cumæan Sibyl, adapted from a male wrestler, Adam and Eve, and other genetic landmarks.

The figure of Adam, a reclining, dormant giant more than thirteen feet long, was painted in three days! The model for this titan was an Italian athlete, but the painting itself has no counterpart in nature. It was fabricated, along with Eve and Noah and the Prophets, from a prophetic vision of superhumanity which the artist unfolded on the ceiling of a church for the inspiration of the world as long as the world holds together.

THE ARTISTS of Florence were concerned with the triumphs and miseries of the human race: the religious convictions of man, his nobility of spirit, his courage, pity and his might; and conversely, his weaknesses and transgressions—the whole gamut of human passions except the light-hearted and pleasurable. In contrast, the artists of Venice were the great decorators of sensuality, the celebrants of a single mood and attitude—the worship of aristocratic splendor and the glittering luxuries peculiar to the courtesan city of the Adriatic. The Venetians were specialists not in the turmoils of the soul, but in the manipulation of light, color and atmosphere, in smooth surfaces and amply rounded forms, the voluptuous side of life which, tempered by time and distance, still seems enchanting and romantic.

The foremost Venetian master was Tiziano Vecellio, known to posterity as Titian, whose art embroiders and reflects the physical harmonies and bacchanalian pursuits immortalized by the city of canals. He was one of the most fortunate of painters, successful in every sense of the word, temperamentally above wasteful introspections—a stock-broker at heart in a community of gilded leaders whose names were inscribed in the Book of Gold, and of kept ladies of culture. He loved the good things of life but never descended to gluttony; an engaging host, he was at ease with kings, blondes and prelates; a hard bargainer, he was at infinite pains to fulfill a contract once he had signed it; a stranger to suffering and emotional tribulations, he painted better as he grew older, and was active to his death in his ninety-ninth year.

Titian was not a native Venetian. He came from the Alpine town of Cadore seventy miles to the north, a steady, talented young painter who was slow to find himself and whose pictures, to the age of thirty-five, were not distinguished for their originality. But when he did find himself, he rose steadily from year to year, and none of the honors of his profession, in ducats or in renown, was denied him.

The tenor of his long career was equable and he conducted his affairs with a commercial shrewdness and political sagacity that precluded the agonies and uncertainties besetting the average artist. By no means a sycophant, he realized how the Venetians esteemed themselves and he portrayed them after a standard of aristocratic splendor that has never been surpassed—or even approached. He had an ironclad rule: never paint an old woman under any circumstances, nor an old man if you can help it, and give your clients the maximum of opulence and appeal—women when they are ripe and ready to conceive and men when they are diplomatists and victors.

Titian catered to church and state in the same mercenary spirit; and bargaining pertinaciously for a sinecure, wangled a broker's patent for himself, the equivalent of official painter with only nominal duties. At forty-eight, he married Cecilia, a barber's daughter, after she had borne him three children, and made an honest woman out of her. Cecilia died five years after the ceremony, and he shed no tears. Instead, he bought a house in the suburbs and established himself on a scale worthy of his position. His studio looked down on the open sea; titled ladies and courtesans were his models, and the kings and princes of Europe were honored to be his guests.

Incorruptible by nature, Titian, with the elastic morality of his day, attached himself for profit to Pietro Aretino, the first of the tribe of publicity agents. Aretino, a master of infamy and a blackmailer who grew fat on the returns from salacious gossip, kept a harem in his palace on the Grand Canal, and made his name hated and feared by all decent people. Through his offices, Titian was guided into the select circles of the European courts, winning the support of the great Emperor Charles V, the patronage of Pope Paul III, and of dukes and duchesses galore.

Aretino's qualities were not confined to the tricks of villainy: he could be generous and humane, and would ride all night to comfort one of the inmates of his harem who was dying of consumption in the uplands; he cared seriously for music and painting and had access to the most desirable patrons, and he was a matchless conversationalist. His loyalty to Titian was the only disinterested attachment of his otherwise shameless career, and while there is no doubt that he enjoyed the prestige of the partnership, he made no attempt to extort money from his friend.

It is possible that he had a crafty respect for the painter's fighting courage—Titian was known to be merciless in his dealings with trouble makers—and it is possible too that he was grateful for the one sincere friendship in a world of enmity and suspicion. Venice, being a liberal city, passed no judgment upon Titian, and thought none the worse of him for hobnobbing with a blackmailer for business reasons as well as social relaxation.

At the end of the day, having finished a piece of invective designed to make some potentate quake with terror—and pay off—Aretino would stand at his window above the Grand Canal exulting in his prowess. He was a burly figure, as you may see in the portraits Titian made of him—a satyr with a splendid beard—thickset and formidable, with the golden chain of knighthood around his neck and a sneering regality in his repulsive face. The shimmering mist dragging over the Canal lifted and an amazing sunset burst upon him.

"Nature," he exclaimed, "the mistress of masters! How miraculous is her brush! How wonderful her pencil! I know that your brush, my friend Titian, is the rival of nature, and that you are her best beloved son!"

A gondola appeared bringing Titian and a plump blonde, and Aretino, after drinking deeply, improvised a toast in honor of the feast, the painter, the blonde, and his own mistress, his favorite Franceschina. And so the night began.

Through the machinations of his publicity agent, Titian painted not only the Emperor Charles V and all his family but also Paul III, while His Holiness was visiting at Ferrara. Finishing the portrait in his studio at Venice, as was his custom, he placed the canvas outside on the terrace to dry; and the passing crowds took off their hats and crossed themselves as if they were in the presence of the Pope himself. For the nuns of Murano he painted an Annunciation, but failing to come to terms with the holy ladies, he sent the picture, on the advice of Aretino, to the Empress, and received, as he had fully expected, a handsome check for the present.

Still more honors awaited him. He was the favorite of Philip II of Spain, and at the age of ninety, sent fifteen canvases to the Spanish court, all the while complaining of his mounting income tax. As a nonagenarian, he took a bolder grip on his brush, and painted with astonishing freedom. He was hard at work on a Pietà in return for space for his own tomb, when the plague stopped his cunning forever.

Titian, as I have indicated, was the matchless portrayer of the external splendor of the world, being totally indifferent to the loftier manifestations of the spirit. In his own special province no man ever painted better, and if you are partial to the gorgeous bloom and fulness of life, he will be your number one painter. *The Man with the Glove,* modeled from the face and figure of a forgotten nobleman, is the quintessence of princeliness; all that is second-rate, or rustic, or boorish, has been eliminated, and the young man is a veritable lord, a pre-Byronic type, broad of shoulder, superior, slightly disdainful, a lady-killer in a million. In the same category is *The Young Englishman,* a wistful, poetic, aristocrat before whom ambitious American and British girls drool and swoon.

He preferred to paint women in the nude and often remained within the bosom of his own family when pressed for models, making his wife sit for studies of mythological heroines, and his strapping daughter, Lavinia, for Venus and Salome. The second wife of the Duke of Ferrara— she was promoted from mistress to wife—posed for a picture sometimes called *Titian's Mistress,* and also sat for the famous *Flora,* the most gracious strumpet in art—an ivory-skinned beauty who somehow carries the seal of her profession. Having addressed his brush to the Duchess of Urbino, wife of one of his richest patrons, and a woman of imperial ugliness, he transformed the haughty client into a superb and dignified piece of humanity. Going further, he depicted her, in *La Bella*, of the Pitti—as the mature image of sensuality and worldliness—and the old dame was ecstatic. There was only one thing more to be done and he was quite capable of doing it—but she was no longer young and was far from shapely. A beautiful nude harlot was paid to pose for the figure and the Duchess's head was annexed to the seductive body. The nude bears the title *Venus of Urbino*, a painting that incurred the righteous indignation of Mark Twain who could stomach the nakedness but not the position of the left hand. "Obscenity!" he exclaimed. "If writers were allowed such license, literature would go to the dogs." Perhaps he was right. The time has come when writers are allowed such privileges—and literature is going into the doghouse.

When Titian was about seventy, he went to Rome at the invitation of Cardinal Farnese. The Pope welcomed him cordially and gave him quarters in the Belvedere of the Vatican, and Michelangelo, curiously enough, treated him with the greatest respect. I say curiously enough because Michelangelo had a low opinion of Venetian art and somewhat cavalierly declared it to be wanting in drawing and spiritual substance.

In Rome, Titian painted a number of things for the Cardinal, and a second portrait of Paul III, one of the most powerful of his works, but receiving nothing for his services except fine words, he returned to Venice. The next year he was summoned to Germany, and there, at the Imperial Court, painted Charles V for the third time—"in bronze armor studded with gold as he was in his old age" —and a host of sovereigns and princes. During one of the ceremonials, the Emperor made Titian ride at his side, and remarked to his courtiers: "I can make as many lords as I wish, but only God can make a Titian."

In the last decade of his life, Titian's art suffered a profound change of approach, both technically and spiritually. The pleasures of the flesh were spent; mistresses were useless, and thoughts of approaching death inspired his brush. He painted Charles V as a scarecrow Don Quixote, a symphony in blood and black, and produced a bacchanal that is far from alluring. Never a religious painter in the Florentine sense, he created for the first and last time, a truly religious work, the *Christ Crowned with Thorns*, and with this dramatic composition entered the hierarchy of the recognized religious masters.

F ROM the fifteenth to the middle of the nineteenth century, it was customary, indeed man-
datory, for artists of all kinds—painters, sculptors,
poets and musicians—to go down to Italy and live
there as long as possible on borrowed money. If
they were painters like Rubens, Poussin, and Sir
Joshua Reynolds, they studied and emulated the
methods of the old masters; if they were poets like
Byron, Shelley and Keats, they drank in the inspiration afforded by the deposits of the highest
culture of the western world.

Thus it happened that the old painting of Italy
established the standards upon which the bulk of
the art of the modern world is based; and even today such showmen as Salvador Dali—the Spaniard
who paints molten watches filled with ants and the
nightmares of surrealism—counsel all beginners to
go back to Leonardo da Vinci and Raphael and
learn the magic secrets of putting paint on canvas.
But there must be a beginning somewhere and one
of the most intelligent of French artists, Delacroix,
asked the question, "But what did the Greeks do
for antiques?"

All of which leads to the question, "What conditions are favorable to the growth and development of art?" I must reply that I do not know, but it requires no special reading of history to discover that the Italians did not produce art by running away from home. On the contrary, they produced it by staying at home and sticking passionately to their own beliefs, habits, and modes of living. In fact, in the palmy days of the Renaissance, Italy was a nest of little States, each of which, no bigger than a man's hand on the map, had its own school of painting that was guarded with inordinate pride.

I mention these matters because, up to this point, we have been dealing with painters universally recognized as the giants of art, and they have been Italians—and if we had not been working in small compass, we might have included fifty instead of only three. But now we proceed northward into new lands and climes, into Germany, Holland, Belgium, and England, and we shall see that the leaders of art in these countries had to compete not only with their own countrymen but also with the authority of the old Italians.

Beginning with Germany in the fifteenth century, we find that two men were forced to consider the effect of their own race and environment on the classic method originated in Italy. One was Albrecht Dürer, and the other was Hans Holbein, the subject of this chapter. Both came to maturity at a portentous hour in the history of German culture: when the Italian Renaissance, in its northward progression, was spreading the humanities of freedom, intellect and scientific curiosity, and when the movement known as the Reformation was resisting religious imagery.

Dürer, though foursquare in his devotion to native sentiments and Protestantism, was a many-sided figure capable of testing the riper culture of the south. He went down to Venice and gathered all his faculties together in a deliberate effort to acquire an Italian style—and almost made it. But it was not until he returned to his home in Nuremberg that he discovered himself, and his efforts to become Italian will be remembered only as intellectual curiosities.

His young contemporary, Holbein, had no intellectual pretensions, and though acquainted with the Italians, never succumbed to their influence. He was a painter pure and simple, and in what he set out to accomplish, remains without many rivals. He formed his art in the Rhine schools of his own country, mastered his craft before he was twenty, and was perhaps the most remarkable portrait painter in Europe. He never gave the Italians more than a passing thought.

Hans Holbein, the Younger, the most gifted member of a family of artists, was a Bavarian German born in the town of Augsburg about 1497. Painting was his trade and with the thoroughness characteristic of his race, he was relentlessly trained as a craftsman both in painting and engraving, and was taught from the beginning to regard human faces as infinitely varied maps and to capture the minute distinctions in features and personalities. At seventeen he was a better artist than his father, and his portraits of the local burgomaster and his frau, done at the age of nineteen, can only be described as minor miracles of workmanship.

In search of a wider outlet for his talents, he wandered to Switzerland where he married a widow to whom he was cruelly unfaithful and generally indifferent. Ambitious and hardboiled, he held his fellow artists in contempt, and though a professed Lutheran, he painted for the Roman Catholics as well, when the stakes were high. The portraits finished during these early years, particularly those of the renowned Dutch scholar Erasmus, then sojourning in Basel, are masterpieces; and his series of woodcuts called *The Dance of Death* holds its own today with the supreme achievements in the field of engraving. When the followers of Martin Luther proscribed religious painting, and the first families had no money for portraits, Holbein went to England as the guest of Sir Thomas More, the Chancellor of Henry VIII.

Two years later, returning to Basel to wind up his affairs, he painted his wife and two children in one of the most touching pictures of German art: his family as he alone knew them, the children with wondering, unhappy faces, the mother with eyelids reddened from weeping. When the iconoclasts, a set of mad reformers, began to confiscate paintings, he hurried off to England and settled there permanently. His old patron, Sir Thomas More, was no longer around, having lost his head by order of the King, but the artist, a shrewd practitioner, was not disheartened. For an organization of German merchants he painted in his most impressive style a likeness of George Gisze, a handsome young man dressed in silks and surrounded by small objects rendered with incredible skill—a vase of carnations, writing materials, keys, scales and letters—one of the most celebrated portraits of the world. The effect was precisely what Holbein had calculated. The young man looked like a prince, and the rich merchants ordered portrait after portrait. They, too, wanted to look like princes.

Eventually, by playing up to the right people, he won the position he coveted most, that of court painter to Henry VIII, a position he clung to the rest of his life and to which, it might be added, he brought eternal glory. He portrayed the King and his courtiers—and his queens and prospective victims—and while acting as matrimonial agent for Henry, turned up in Basel arrayed in silks and fine linen, and supercilious to everyone. Bidding farewell to his wretched family, he hurried back to the

British court, and four years afterward, was carried off by the plague in his middle forties.

Holbein could paint anything or anybody with uniform brilliancy, but seldom bothered with sitters of inferior birth or humble station. Make no mistake, however, about this German: he was a great artist, as well as a cold-blooded schemer, and never once stooped to a slipshod or unworthy performance. He was the most detached and objective of all artists; that is to say, he kept himself out of the picture so far as it is humanly possible, revealing the character and physiognomy of the subject to perfection, but taking pains to exclude his own feelings and preferences. Thus it was that he created, not a collection of types, but of individuals one and all, specific persons like Erasmus and the King, with their occupations, virtues and shortcomings fully realized. At the same time, of course, his pictures of men and women are unmistakably Holbein's. They are calm and self-possessed like the artist who made them; they never flinch, nor smile, and they are seldom exhibited in moments of inward turmoil or external action.

The court of Henry VIII, with its supernumeraries and hangers-on, lives in the portraits of Hans Holbein. He left to posterity a period of history more beautifully and convincingly created than anything done in words by professional historians. Behold the beefy, gross, sensual and intelligent monarch himself, and a retinue of lords, ladies, knights, brides and bootlickers! Not a crew of stuffed doublets and crinolines, but living men and women presented without flattery or malice, without lying or counterfeit charms. There they stand in all their solemnity: *Robert Cheseman, The King's Falconer, The Archbishop of Canterbury, Lady Audley*—so British you can catch the accent, *Lady Guildford,* fat and arrogant, *Anne Boleyn, Jane Seymour, The Earl of Surrey,* with the wappy jaws of the cockney, delicate miniatures of *Edward, Prince of Wales,* and a gallery of others.

At the King's behest he went to Brussels to take a likeness of Princess Christina of Denmark, a sixteen-year-old widow; and from a sketch and an oil study of the head made in three hours, constructed one of the loveliest of portraits, a slender young lady all in black, and very gentle and appealing, but not prettified or oversweetened. Henry instantly proposed marriage but the girl widow turned him down, saying that "she would gladly have consented to be his queen, if the Good Lord had but given her two heads, one for the King to chop off, and one to wear home again."

On a similar mission to Flanders, Holbein painted one of his most popular canvases, *Anne of Cleves,* called "the playing-card Queen," from its decorative resemblance to the royal lady of the deck. Anne of Cleves had no glamor but when Henry filled his eyes with the gold and red splendor of the painting, he sent word that he desired her for his wife and queen.

On meeting her at the boat, he was so shocked by her plain dull face that he forgot to hand over the gift he had brought. It was too late now to back away and he went through with the cere-mony, only to have Parliament annul the marriage. Anne did not seem to mind. She was not revenge-ful and not very bright, and when the King gave her a home in England, and an allowance and a new dress every day, she counted herself the most fortunate of women.

No artist ever got more out of a model than Hol-bein did. He could paint the figure with ease, but his primary concern was with the face. He did not seek to photograph the face, but to seize upon its significant features and peculiarities—to model and outline and underscore the basic structure; to de-fine with absolute precision the depth and turn of the eye-socket, the curve of the mouth and the line of the head in profile—all these to build up a perfect likeness and a lasting study of character. He had taste and style—rare qualities in a German —a fine sense of color and exquisite craftsmanship— with none of the sentimentality of the German school. Today, with portraiture in low estate, art and the world could use a man like Holbein, a painter capable of showing up the face, the fa-cetious, brutal, befuddled and tragical faces of the men who rule the human race.

Plate 9

RUBENS
Artist and His First Wife

Plate 10   Judgement of Paris (DETAIL)

RUBENS
Portrait of a Woman

REMBRANDT
Death of the Virgin

Plate 13

REMBRANDT
Rembrandt and Wife

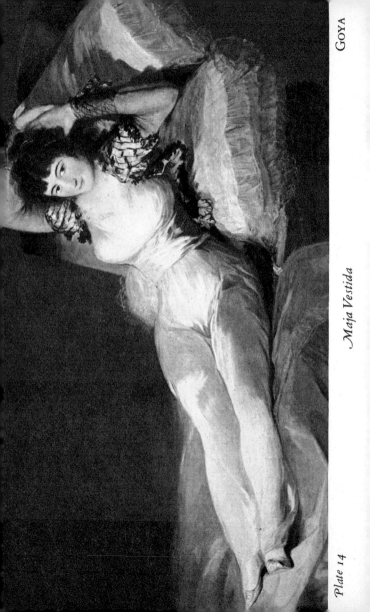

Maja Vestida

Plate 14

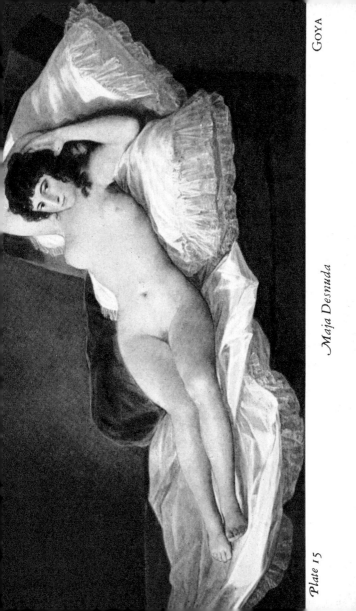

Maja Desnuda

Plate 15

Plate 16

VELASQUEZ
Infanta

To NAME the greatest of all artists would be no more than an expression of individual preferences, but when it comes to the greatest of painters, there is not much room for speculation. The man was Peter Paul Rubens, whose command over the visual medium—his ability to portray the human figure in every conceivable posture and to relate figures one to another in surging, intricate compositions—was so phenomenal as to invite comparison, not with the members of his own profession but with the greatest master of words the world has seen, William Shakespeare.

His father, a doctor of laws, and his mother, a tapestry weaver, were of solid Flemish stock, but the boy happened to be born in a town west of Cologne where his parents had sought refuge until the Duke of Alba had finished with the Netherlands. When the Rubens family returned to Antwerp, the Spanish fury had accomplished its purpose, slaughtering multitudes of innocent burghers and razing cities and towns with an intensive thoroughness not repeated until the invasions of the modern Germans. Nevertheless, the mother of

Peter Paul Rubens, a remarkable woman, took care to see that her son was properly educated. The boy spoke German and Flemish from infancy, Latin under the tutelage of his father, and French after serving as page to a princess. At the outset of his professional career, along with numerous other attainments, he was fluent in seven tongues.

He began to draw in his childhood at Cologne; at thirteen avowed his intention of becoming an artist; studied with three Flemish painters, and at twenty-three, already a leader and superbly equipped mentally and physically for the superhuman labors associated with his name, departed for Venice on horseback. An artist with the graces of a prince and the discretion of a gentleman, he was immediately snapped up by the Duke of Mantua, for whom, besides his routine duties as court painter, he journeyed to Spain on a diplomatic mission. At the end of nine years of study and incessant productivity, he returned to Antwerp to bury his mother.

His fame had traveled before him. Rubens was welcomed by the bigwigs of the city and named official painter to the viceroys, Albert and Isabella. The field of art, devastated and wide open, was his for the taking, but three years went by—years in which, as he said, he again warmed his blood at the Flemish hearth—before he got the Italians out of his system and discovered the originality at the bottom of his powers.

To his palatial house in Antwerp, with its galleries and formal gardens, journeyed the most eminent men in Europe; and his vast studio became the art center of the Continent, sending out under his direction more than three thousand canvases, some entirely by his own hand and certified accordingly, others executed in collaboration from his designs. Contrary to the impression created by the prevalence of nude women in his pictures, he was strictly monogamous and there is no compromising gallantry against his name.

His first wife was Isabella Brandt, not quite eighteen when he took her, strong, fine looking and built on Flemish contours. During fifteen years of happy married life, his production was enormous, the famous picture factory running at full blast, and the plundered churches of Flanders were stocked with large-scale masterpieces. Small jobs irked him, and he wrote, "There is no task too large for my brush, but I can't paint little curiosities." The curiosities—the ordinary portraits and the dead game and fishes—were relegated to his subordinates.

For Maria de' Medici, fat daughter of a fat Florentine banker, he painted the mural decorations now in the Louvre; eighteen panels thirteen feet by ten, three canvases, thirteen by twenty-four feet, and a number of eight-foot portraits—a colossal undertaking which stands in the history of mural painting with Giotto's Chapel at Padua and the Sistine Chapel of Michelangelo. His wife died and "to ease the sorrows of the heart," he said, he rode off in midsummer over the dusty mountains to Spain on an ambassadorial errand. This discharged, he returned by way of England where he contracted at a staggering price to decorate the banqueting chamber of Whitehall for Charles I.

In Antwerp again, a lonely widower of fifty-three he married Helen Fourment, barely sixteen, the youngest and fairest of seven sisters all famous for their beauty, and his creative energies flamed with unprecedented brilliancy. On one consignment, he delivered 112 paintings to the King of Spain, pausing in his labors to run over to Holland to pacify the angry Dutch. Sick of politics and the drain on his hospitality, he bought the Château de Steen, a country estate, for a sum equivalent to $125,000, and living there in the clement months, painted some of the most spacious and serene and powerful landscapes in existence. But his giant activities were soon ended. His old enemy, the gout—an affliction he didn't deserve, for he was a temperate man—returned to cause him acute suffering. In his sixty-third year, his heart failed him, and the religious orders of Antwerp celebrated seven hundred Masses for the consolation of his expansive soul.

Unexcelled in portraiture, Rubens attracted hundreds of models including kings and dukes, queens and infantas, his wives and his nine children, and his in-laws. One of his first great portraits—and it is a beauty—presents himself and his bride, Isabella Brandt, in all their health and finery: Rubens with a trim beard, a curled moustache, and gorgeous attire—a doublet of yellow-green, black velvet breeches, orange stockings and a Henry Quatre hat. Isabella wears a black jacket, a blue satin bodice embroidered in gold, a violet skirt and yellow petticoat—and the two are holding hands.

Time and again he painted his children, painted and drew them from infancy to adolescence and made them models of youth and art. There is something of his wives in all his women, whether they were posed as Christian saints or mythological goddesses. His first wife may be identified as the Magdalene in *The Descent from the Cross*, and Helen, his second, is the model for his most wonderful nudes. "She did not blush when I took up my brush," he said; and she was exposed to the world in unabashed, naked womanhood—a northern goddess, large and meaty, but stately in her strength and health. You may see her in *The Fur Coat* at Vienna, a semi-nude portrait; as Venus in *The Judgment of Paris*, in London; and as the lady on the left in *The Three Graces of Madrid*, perhaps the best nudes of their kind ever composed. She has blue eyes, golden hair, a straight nose and small voluptuous mouth—and a figure which painters love but which modern women would starve and constrict and girdle to death.

Rubens loved the nude as an organic fact and accepted its challenge without trepidation, undue excitement or any thoughts of exhibitionism. His undraped women are as healthy and chaste as his wives were; in truth, most of them were modeled, as I have said, from his wives; and his sexual appetites being amply satisfied in real life, he had no occasion to resort to the imaginary compensations of art. All his nudity is clean and pure and undisguised. He could not have said what he had to say with thin women; for his is a lush and burgeoning world with no room for the thin and the stunted. Rubens would have loved the tendency of our American women towards nakedness, both formally and in relaxing pursuits, but he would deplore the fetish of lean flesh and the elaborate aids to simulate emaciation. He might conclude that the end and aim of American ingenuity is to constrict the female rump and to provide a matrix for the mammary glands. And those streamlined professional models, those one-dimensional, overpaid creatures, would offer him nothing useful, until he had fattened them up and made them look like functioning females.

REMBRANDT died in 1669, the last of the giants, battered but unbeaten, and of all the men of art worth writing about, the closest to the heart of humanity. As a psychological record of man's rise and fall, and the path of the spirit towards complete freedom, he painted himself again and again. Everybody knows the Dutchman's face: in youth a little proud of early success, in old age, seamed and kindly—the eyes bleary from excessive use of the etcher's needle, and too much Holland gin—but direct and at peace with the world. And his pictures, though intrinsically Dutch and local, will never become old-fashioned or dead material for the doctors of art. They were made for mankind and they are within the grasp of the humblest layman. No technical barriers block the way of appreciation and today, in a world struggling with bellicose materialism, they offer the highest rewards to all who will pause to consider them.

Rembrandt was born in Leyden, in 1606. His father, a miller who ground malt for beer, was fairly prosperous; his mother, a baker's daughter, was a woman of more than average intelligence.

There were four older brothers, all mediocrities, and one sister to whom he was devoted. It was clear from the beginning that the youngest son was not destined for humdrum occupations. He was absorbed in the Bible, which his God-fearing mother read to him in those long northern evenings; and the good woman, under the illusion that he would grow up to be a great preacher, or, as second choice, a surgeon, sent him, at the age of fourteen, to the University of Leyden. The experiment did not pan out. Books, the Bible excepted, bored the headstrong boy; Latin was a nuisance, and he filled his notebooks with drawings. At the close of a year, he withdrew from academic rigmarole, and signed up with a local painter.

Like every artist of the first magnitude, he proved his extraordinary capacities in his teens, and so remarkable was his progress, that in three years, he was sent to Amsterdam to study with the renowned Lastman. It was an unfortunate venture: the renowned teacher was a conceited pedant, and Rembrandt soon left him, but not before he had explored a new method of illuminating pictures by startling oppositions of lights and darks. The method was an Italian invention, but the Dutch artist, in the course of time, so refined and modified it as to make it synonymous with his own name.

Before he was twenty-one he was a celebrity in his home town, and the life of a local art circle. Once he had tested the fruits of professionalism, he worked harder than ever, by daylight at his painting, by night at his etching. He began to make money, and to spend it, and at twenty-six, made his home in Amsterdam for good. That city, in 1632, having escaped the horrors of war, was a thriving community of orderly, decent money-grubbers; and the artist, immediately on his arrival, was commissioned to paint a memorial to the surgeon's guild. The result was a painting which may be seen in doctors' offices throughout the world, *The Anatomy Lesson*, seven bearded doctors and a doctor-professor posing round a corpse.

Thenceforth, for ten years, Rembrandt was not only a popular favorite but a man of wealth, foremost in his profession and virtually without competitors. When his dealer brought to his studio a girl of twenty named Saskia Van Uylenborch, a blonde, sweet-faced orphan, he wooed and won her against the protests of skinflint relatives who thought the painter low-bred and inferior to the girl. His wife loved fine clothes and jewels; he, in turn, could not resist antiques and authentic Italian masterpieces, and between them, the money he made was quickly put into circulation.

During these busy productive years, three children were born and buried in infancy, and the artist moved to a house in the ghetto to observe at firsthand the refugees who seemed to him to personify the characters in the dramatic stories of the Old Testament. A fourth child arrived, a son, and the son lived—to his great delight, but the mother, never strong, declined and died. His grief was intensified by the rejection of *The Night Watch*, a group portrait of some swashbucklers who counted on a more flattering treatment. The painting, too bold and original for conventional clients, pleased nobody and marked the end of Rembrandt's popularity. Moreover, on top of it all, his son's old nurse hailed him into court on the charge of adultery and he was ordered to increase her allowance.

Undaunted, he produced some of his greatest paintings, and that incomparable etching, *Christ Healing the Sick*. His life was made more bearable by the presence of his young housekeeper, Hendrickje Stoffels, dark and sad of eye, with a blooming complexion, and a well-rounded figure. She could neither read nor write, but she had the character of a saint and a loyalty that no misfortune could diminish. Their first child died at birth, but the second, whom he named Cornelia after his mother, survived the overworked artist.

From now on, it was a race against time. Commissions ceased, he borrowed money and could not repay it, and his consort Hendrickje was helpless in the impending storm. Her own child was properly cared for; Saskia's child was growing stronger; the master's work was wonderful beyond belief—and she did not understand designing creditors. A general showdown ensued; the painter was declared bankrupt, and his house, together with most of his personal effects, passed into the possession of a shoemaker.

The evicted giant was not embittered. He invited the auctioneer to an inn for a drink; borrowed a press and pulled off a number of etchings which he sold to dealers who took advantage of his poverty; and moved to the lowest quarter of the slums. Debt-ridden and shabby, he soon became wholly dependent on his son, but the light of his genius shone out with increasing majesty. In most cases, when a man grows slovenly in his habits and his dress, his spirit becomes correspondingly shabby and second-rate; but Rembrandt, as tribulations piled up, bore all with equanimity and looked upon the worst of his fellow men without malice or resentment—one with the pure of heart, an emancipated soul, if ever one lived.

With the purest sympathy for all God's creatures, an understanding born of toil and domestic tragedy, Rembrandt went on working, and brought into being works of art which no one would believe possible unless we had living, tangible proof of their existence. His wants were meager—cheese and herring and plenty of gin—and the colored mud and oil of the painter's palette—and, of course, the responses of Hendrickje. He squatted by a window above an old canal and painted a portrait of his ailing son. The young man died, and the old man, in his best rags, a fur coat smeared with paint, and his bearing erect and stately, followed the body to the grave. He had conquered his difficulties long before death put an end to them, and when it was all over and the funeral procession wound its way through the dismal streets, the loafers of the quarter whispered that the deceased had once been a famous man in Amsterdam.

Rembrandt painted the faces of men, women, and children, not merely to transcribe a likeness, but to show how the human countenance reflects the resignation, the bewilderment and the tragedy of what we are pleased to call the inner man, or the soul. There are no happy faces in his gallery of portraits, the one exception being the jolly nuptial picture of himself with Saskia on his knee; and he constructed the human head like an inspired mason, of tones of light and dark translated into their color equivalents—light and dark transfigured, Lord knows how, into massive components that seem to be dug out of mysterious mixtures of radiance and shadow. His first model was himself, a bull-necked fellow before a mirror; and his last model was himself, a beatific old hulk whom he presented, in strokes as broad as the swipes of a trowel, as a grotesque mask of colored mud laughing at those who had tried to lick him.

He persuaded his father to pose for him and portrayed the wrinkled little miller in robes and a turban, and gave him a Biblical name; his sister sat to him and lives on as the Virgin or a fine lady, and his mother as the very effigy of forbearance. Impelled by compassion to the lower orders, for his art seems to bind together all suffering mortals, he drew and etched the deformed and blind and crippled soldiers who wandered over Holland after the wars, begging for bread. In his early prodigal years, rich merchants and arrogant brewers sat to him for money—and his portraits of them are not too distinguished—but at the same time, he was painting *Diana at the Bath*, an interpretation of an old crone who came to his studio, a frightening thing with hanging breasts and legs cut by garters. He painted the frail and tender Saskia at twenty-one, when she accepted his advances, and time and again during their life together: as Flora, the goddess of spring, as an irresistible creature with a red flower, and naked, as Suzanna; and he painted his son and his son's wife.

The models for his religious pictures, and he was the last of the great religious painters—and by long odds the most human—were his own family and Portuguese Jews who roamed the ghetto of Amsterdam. The Italians looked upon life from afar and created holy paintings of transcendental qualities; whereas Rembrandt, observing the world as man to man, produced the most intimate and moving and dramatic of Biblical pictures. A young Portuguese Jew posed for his conception of Christ in *The Supper at Emmaus*, and in the etching, *Healing the Sick;* and these two pictures, in their uncanny revelation of the world that all of us, in our ethereal moments seem to be conscious of, represent the topmost flights of imaginative conviction.

Approaching the final bout with paint and gin, and fighting the inexorable toll of sorrow and overwork, he gave the world his portrait of the *Syndics*, a group of merchants who are closer to the eternal scheme of things than are the apostles of Italian art in their flowing robes. And he gave us his pictures of Hendrickje whom he loved more than worldly recognition and fine gold, sometimes as a tested, upright woman ready to stand at the judgment bar of God, again naked as *Bathsheba* or as a *Woman Bathing,* but always as a woman whose beauty lies not in outward graces, but as the embodiment of a person for whom life holds no terrors.

Unconsciously perhaps, Rembrandt painted all his faces as old faces, for he had no use for models until experience and sacrifice impressed themselves on their visages. He loved to think that every man and woman can conquer his afflictions in one way or another, and his portraits represent the best the human race can offer, after it has divested itself of the raiment of materialism and rankling pretensions.

TECHNICALLY, Velasquez could paint as well, or better, than the best of his profession, and if you prefer in art pictures exquisitely rendered by a brush dipped in light and air, quiet pictures devoid of soul troubles and the dramatic impact of a strong personality, then the Spaniard is your man. He could do no wrong, and aware of his limitations, left the profound states of the soul to artists like Leonardo da Vinci, Michelangelo and Rembrandt. You need not be told, if you have examined his paintings, that his life was singularly free from the trials and vicissitudes which add color and depth to an artist's handiwork.

He was, to be exact, a Portuguese aristocrat born in Sevilla in 1599, and in his thirteenth year apprenticed to a painter of some prominence from whom he learned next to nothing. His next teacher was Pacheco, a scholar and a good companion with a comely daughter named Juana—and before he was twenty Velasquez had married the girl. The most promising painter in Spain, he went to Madrid to seek his fortune, or more exactly, to use political influence to obtain an appointment with

King Philip, the new sovereign. He won the young King's favor by an equestrian portrait, was given the post of royal painter, and for thirty-six years, or the rest of his life, was retained by the awkward monarch. His salary was pitifully low, and he was graded socially with the idiots, dwarfs and minor parasites of the court, but the perquisites were unfailing and abundant. He was given a studio in the royal palace, was honored by bales of cast-off clothing from the King, and by daily baskets of bread and wine from the Queen.

Velasquez was perfectly contented. For the successful prosecution of his art he needed no new experiences—nothing, in fact, but a model. Twice, in compliance with royal suggestions, he went to Italy, and in his last years, as valet to the King's bedchamber and Marshall of the Palace—the supervisor of festivals and weddings—he added a few pesos to his purse; but the extra-pictorial strain was too much for him, and he died of a heart attack while preparing a matrimonial fête for the Infanta Maria Teresa. His spouse, having nothing to live for, died eight days afterward.

This clear-sighted Portuguese did not inquire into the character of his models, nor was he influenced by one kind of life over another. The royal family whom he portrayed under compulsion afforded him no more inspiration than the buffoons and sightless idiots maintained by the Hapsburgs to relieve the boredom of the court. In his heart, and so far as his talents were concerned, he did not care whether his subjects were regal, or whether they were dwarfs or skinned rabbits. He put them down on canvas, with uncanny precision and dexterity, in blended tones of grey and rose and silver, and they excited him no more than pieces of still life.

Philip IV did nothing of distinction in his whole life and a more unkingly wretch never sat on a hard throne, but the Hapsburg lives on and on in the canvases of his painter. Velasquez first took him as a knock-kneed monarch of eighteen and thereafter, year after year, he delineated with a brush that became more and more cunning—the dead-fish eyes, the underhung jaw, the long yellow hair and the vacuous gaze of the man whom wanton fortune had made a king. You may see King Philip in many museums, and he is a perfect example of how the artist by his technical graces can raise an unsightly model into the realm of the beautiful.

As a painter of the figure, or combinations of figures, Velasquez was a novice compared to Rubens, and in his two attempts at large-scale group pictures, his trick was to avoid action and difficulties of posture and to rely on multiple portraiture. *The Surrender of Breda* is one, a scene in which all the participants are huddled in the foreground and photographed in pigment. The other is *The Maids of Honor*, the artist's studio as seen by himself in a mirror with numerous royal visitors including the Infanta and her attendants, dogs and dwarfs, and the King and Queen dimly reflected in a glass on the wall, in a complicated lighting.

How a man of his ability could have been content to slave day after day as the King's prisoner is something of a mystery, since artists, as a rule, are bold and rebellious human beings, and not disposed to accept the fetters of conventionality or incarceration. Velasquez, to be truthful, was a scientific mechanism, and not once did he fawn upon his superiors or lie about them in paint. He expended his talents on the poet Góngora, the Spanish exponent of preciosity; on various courtiers and slaveys; on the Queen of Spain and the King, and Prince Baltazar Carlos astride a stuffed horse, and the little Infanta with her greensick face and eyes touched by incipient madness. Only once did he essay the nude, *The Venus with the Mirror*, a job that does him no great credit.

In his own way, and the ways of art are as various as the personality of the creators, Velasquez was one of the masters. While in Rome, he painted Innocent X, a portrait of unbelievable proficiency, and when the Italian connoisseurs looked upon the solid likeness fashioned out of tones of impalpable thinness, they exclaimed, "It is made out of nothing, but there it is, His Holiness!"

A PEASANT with brute strength and the audacity of genius, Goya climbed to the peak of his profession, and when the revolutionary spirit of France swept across Europe, he became, temperamentally, at least, a part of it and the forerunner of the new freedom in painting. As a man of action, he had ferocious instincts and the vitality to gratify them; as an artist, he was endowed not only with an aptitude for drawing, but with a mind—one of the few first-rate minds of his generation. He dug fearlessly into the superstitions and corruptions of his country and at his death in his eighty-second year, he had, in the rôle of social historian, painted a comprehensive picture of the period.

He was born in a mountain village of one hundred inhabitants; worked with his brothers and his sister in the parched fields until a stroke of fortune ended his misery. The parish priest, so the story runs, caught him drawing on the village walls with a lump of charcoal; found him a wealthy patron, and at fourteen the boy was sent to Saragossa to learn painting. From this point, footloose and unrestrained, he set out on his picaresque journey through the violence of his times; and he hurried from one form of art to another, as he plunged headlong into one form of life after another. Variously gifted, as artist, singer, swordsman and gangster, he was, at nineteen, credited with all sorts of foolhardy adventures, and the Goya legend had its beginning. At his death, the legend had grown to epic proportions, and to this day the facts and the fiction have not been successfully separated. It is enough to say, that however hair-raising, or scandalous the deed, he was capable of it, anyway.

It is told that he left for Madrid in a hurry, after a murderous brawl, to escape the wrath of the Inquisitors; and it is known that in Madrid he consorted with bullfighters and had some standing as an amateur toreador. In trouble at the capital, he fled to Rome where he supported himself as a freelance portraitist. He had no special reverence for Italian art, but the gay life of Rome—the carnivals, prostitutes and the underworld—excited his imagination, and the Goya legend increased in boldness and color. It is said that he carved his name in the lantern of St. Peter's and that he broke into a nunnery to kidnap a young lady who had resisted his advances.

He returned to Spain to see his parents, and to get a foothold as an artist. Not being a religious painter, and unsparing of hypocrites, high or low, he was not very prosperous before his thirty-fifth year. At twenty-nine he married the sister of a well-known painter, and the long-suffering woman, after the Spanish mandate, stayed at home in a state of chronic pregnancy while he lived dangerously among the gypsies, dancing girls, *putas* and bullfighters. Twenty children were born, a sickly lot, for all his virility, only one reaching maturity; and the artist-father, addicted to debauches of working and eating, was in poor health throughout the latter half of his life.

When Charles IV came to the throne, he was appointed one of the court painters and immediately got into hot water. A series of etchings, *Los Caprichos*, in which the throne, the law and the army were satirized mercilessly, seemed to delight the victims, but when he ventured to ridicule the priests, the long arm of the Inquisition reached out and only the King's intervention saved his skin. In gratitude, Goya decorated the church of San Antonio de la Florida on royal property near Madrid with one hundred figures larger than life and all done in three months!

As first court painter, Goya painted the royal family and the court attendants, and nonofficially the dignitaries of Spain, civil and military alike. It was the period of his finest portraiture, but life was using him ruthlessly. His favorite son was good for nothing, and his favorite woman, the Duchess of Alba, died in 1802. Surly and unyielding, and half-deaf, he lived on, painting more beautifully with age. Surviving one regime after the other and loathing them all, he fraternized with the invading Bonapartes, and when they were thrown out, managed to get into the good graces of Ferdinand who said: "You deserve exile, but you are an artist, and I will forget everything."

At seventy-two, he sequestered himself in a house on the outskirts of Madrid, the deaf man's villa, it was called, and relieved himself by decorating the walls with huge and grotesque figures. He made etchings of the bull ring; visited France, with the King's permission, and instantly recognized the artists who have lasted, and then, his leave extended, repaired to Bordeaux. There, in exile, half-blind and hard of hearing, he died and left no successors.

Goya's models ranged from aristocrats to beggars, from his own family to the royal house, from the bull ring and the battlefield to the kingdom of monsters. He painted and etched his own head—thick-necked and sensual—and his woebegone wife; and his children and grandchildren, and many other youngsters delineated with affection and an insight born of vast experience. In his hands, Maria Luisa is revolting, and the wonder is that he was not hanged or fired for his uncompromising truthfulness. He exhibited her foul body in an etching with the title, *"She Says Yes to Anyone"*; and in the group picture of *Charles IV and His Family*, she stands erect and unsightly with the King and a dozen other members of a family of eyesores. The group portrait is a brutal exercise in satirical biography, and led Gautier to remark that "the King looks like the grocer who has won the big lottery prize, with his family around him."

A defiant soul, he excoriated hypocrites and phonies in high position—and occasionally his satire was misdirected and his operations unnecessary. In the murals of the Church of San Antonio de la Florida, he flaunted recognizable likenesses of fashionable harlots insidiously rouged and flirting with well-known fops. At the other extreme, when the French came and slaughtered the populace at the city gate, he recorded the massacre in his most brilliantly savage style in the *Execution after the Second of May*, a picture to freeze your soul.

Of all the women in his life, the Duchess of Alba was his favorite. He may even have loved her, for her face haunted him and there is something of the Duchess in all his portraits of women. She was a *maja*, a gay lady, or more than gay, and a patron of bullfighters. Goya met her during the days of his first important commission, the tapestry designs, and immediately found a place for her in one of the cartoons as a young girl struggling with gallants. As their intimacy ripened he presented her more formally in full-length studies and she came to his studio—alone—and when a woman does that in Spain, she is given an ugly name.

"The Duchess of Alba," wrote an infatuated French marquis, "has not a hair on her head that does not arouse desire. Nothing on earth is as lovely as she is, and it is impossible to surpass her." Yet Goya, when the flame was dim, put her into his etching of the two-faced woman and called the plate *Dream of Lies and Inconstancy*.

Her name is indissolubly connected with two of his masterpieces, the *Majas*, nude and covered. Certain Castillians, out to repair the defunct glory of the Albas, insist that the Duchess had not posed for the *Majas*, but the face is there, and the figure is there, and the paintings were in her collection at her death. The canvases are equally seductive and identical in the attitude of the figure, but with a difference: in one the model wears thin, skintight breeches; in the other, she wears nothing.

In his old age, Goya said, "The dream of reason produced monsters," and he fixed his mind's eye on hideous creatures to symbolize the human race that had gone to hell. He filled his pictures with sinister conceptions to reduce his spleen: giant birds croaking, a shriveled idiot among bags of gold, a corpse rising from the tomb and scratching the word "nothing" in the earth.

L ONDON, in the first half of the eighteenth century, was a city of commercialized vice and
beastly recreations. Dueling, whoring, bearbaiting
and cockfighting were the sports of gentlemen,
with another carnal diversion, the seduction of ser-
vant girls, sanctioned by constant practice among
the rakes of higher station. It was a rough-and-
tumble age, the upper classes as devoid of culture
as Saxon swineherds, and duped by foreign sharp-
ers of fancy assumptions; the lower classes flock-
ing to public hangings as connoisseurs today assem-
ble to enjoy the flattening of prizefighters and the
stabbing of bulls; and all classes wallowing in gin,
the national beverage. At night, no one was safe
in the fogs, unless attended by a bodyguard to beat
off the attacks of Irish bullies out to amuse themselves by knocking pedestrians into insensibility.

Starving penny-a-liners and shilling prostitutes
cohabited in the garrets of Grub Street; art was
controlled by auctioneers and black marketeers
of old masters stolen from Italy; and the common
man, as always, had to fight for victuals. This sordid description, however, was not the whole story.

In this tough, bawdy age lived a coterie of intelligent men who contributed to the glory that was England, two-fisted men who worked hard and drank heavily: Jonathan Swift, creator of Lemuel Gulliver; Samuel Johnson, essayist and lexicographer; Henry Fielding, dramatist and novelist; David Garrick, actor; Isaac Newton, scientist; and William Hogarth, painter and engraver.

Hogarth, born in London in 1697, was a true metropolitan who loved the city despite its cutthroats and venal practitioners of art and sex, and no form of life escaped his scrutiny or turned his formidable stomach. You would find him at fairs and taverns, peep-shows and cockfights, election riots and country dances, and you would see him, sketchbook in hand, at public executions. In his youth he was apprenticed to an engraver, and in his twenties, as a commercial artist, designed all sorts of advertisements and tradesmen's cards, which are now collectors' items. At the same time he worked diligently at the hardest problems of his profession, drawing and painting and training his mind and hand for the works that put him above and apart from other British artists.

After eloping with the handsome daughter of a prominent painter, his teacher, Hogarth bent his back to convince the painter that he could support the girl in decency. "My picture is my stage and my men and women my players," he said, and thereupon, reviving the storytelling picture, produced a work which made him the talk of the town. It was called *A Harlot's Progress*, the narrative, in a sequence of paintings, of Moll Hackabout, a pretty country girl of unstable virtue in London. Outsmarting the academic royalists who snubbed him because he did not paint pseudo-classical contraptions in the grand style, he engraved his pictures and the sale of the prints netted him a tidy sum. His first narrative was followed by *The Rake's Progress*, a play in eight scenes unfolding the devious career of a spendthrift who revels in whores, gambles and gets locked up for debt, and dies in Bedlam. It was a better job than the mishaps of the harlot, but dealing with the upper crust and with a man's vagaries, was not so popular.

While engaged in these original sequences, Hogarth participated in many enlightening enterprises; building a foundling hospital for the super-abundance of British bastards; operating an art school—one of the few civilized schools in history; and fighting impostors in every field. His third and best dramatic narrative, *Marriage à la Mode*, reveals the scandals of a titled pair: their dissipations, adulteries and deaths, but it was not received with noticeable applause, and the patrons of art, swayed by the counterfeit Italian style of Reynolds and his minions, passed the word along that it was vulgar and irrelevant. The last decade of his life was enlivened by quarrels and controversies, which never failed to restore his equanimity. He wrote a searching book on beauty, and died of enlargement of the arteries at the age of sixty-seven. Before it was all over, he remarked, "I have gone through life pretty much to my own satisfaction."

This sturdy, beef-eating, blue-eyed Englishman was one of the most versatile and accomplished of northern artists—one of the big men of art, I mean, born in a country not bordering on the Mediterranean. He had a large-size, healthy hatred for a lot of things: white slavers, vote-selling, Frenchmen and gin-drunkards, to name a few; but unlike Swift, he was not a hypochondriac who depicted man as lower than the Yahoo. He loved the beautiful women of England and painted them as human beings, not as duchesses and highborn ladies; and he was at home with the genuine leaders of England on one hand and with the sons of honest toil on the other. Besides, he had a rollicking sense of humor that saved him from sentimentality and when his humor carried him into black-and-white satire, he made pictures with a graver which, like the pen of Mark Twain, was warmed in the fires of hell.

As an example of his creative power, take him in his fiftieth year, when he crossed the Channel and was unjustly arrested for sketching at the seaport's gate. The outrage stung him to the quick, and from sketches done on the spot, he painted *The Gate of Calais*, one of his masterpieces. It is a little scene at the entrance of the city: a porter struggling under the weight of a joint of beef which a fat priest is about to embrace, two emaciated guardsmen grinning pitiably at the sight of food and in the background, the artist plying his trade. Some years ago in London, I examined this canvas in the company of a distinguished French artist who spoke wisely of the design and the quality of the handling of the paint, and then, without warning, burst into a fit of rage. "It is a lie," he yelled. "France never starved her soldiers!"

Probably no other Englishman worked so ardently from his experiences or chose his models so unfailingly from real life and not from the professional posers who stand like dummies in the studio. In one of his paintings, a young girl points to her swollen middle while the rake, or rat, who is the author of her shame, hands her a coin. In another, an engraving called *Gin Lane*, he brings together the bloated jocularity of hard drinkers, the open love-making of the lower classes, and on the wretched side, the horrors of habitual guzzling, with an old hag leering at her naked brat and over the arch of a gin-mill the inscription: "Drunk for a penny; dead drunk for twopence; clean straw for nothing."

The whole of England inspired him—the grim, the sweet, the coarse, the cruel, the lusty and the tender. His portraits are the flowers of British art, characterizations of able-bodied men and beautiful women, one of them, *The Shrimp Girl*, surpassing in delicacy and deftness of execution the French painters who are famous for such virtues. He painted himself with his dog and his easel; his sister Ann, his servants, and many Britishers of distinction: *Quin, the Actor, Garrick and Mrs. Garrick, Peg Woffington,* and the gifted reprobate *Lord Lovat.* On the day that Lord Lovat was hanged, Hogarth attended the picnic, and sold engravings of the overnourished culprit among the waiting spectators.

He painted election riots and swarms of Englishmen, singly and in elaborate composition, the fat along with the lean, and the stately next to the lawless. Hogarth revived the pictorial narrative and put the art of England on its feet, but not one of his successors has rivaled him in those attainments linking his name with the leading figures of his age. His influence on black-and-white art has been continuous and fertilizing and in contemporary America has had a fine effect on such good men as John Sloan and Reginald Marsh.

It is a far cry from the magic of Leonardo da Vinci to the Saxon graces of Hogarth, but the Englishman has his own magic—less elevated than the Italian brand but more human, and of magnetic pungency. He fashioned his various characters with benevolence and humor and graced them with the magic of his personality.

WILLIAM BLAKE's experiences with the supernatural began in his earliest childhood. At the age of four he saw God's face against the windowpane and shrank back in terror; at a still tender age he surprised a flock of angels swinging from the boughs of a tree; and one summer day came home with the story that he had met Ezekiel wandering in an open field. These spiritual adventures increased in range and significance as he grew older and eventually constituted a life more real to him than the pragmatic routine of gaining a livelihood. He became the foremost visionary in Western art—one of the few worth looking at—and a book illustrator and designer of strange and inimitable powers.

He was born in London, in 1757, the son of a poor hosier of mystical inclinations himself and thus not hostile to the boy's commerce with the world of the spirits, nor to his ambition to study painting. But the family was large and unable to afford the luxury of educating a painter, and as the next best thing, William was articled to an engraver. His apprenticeship of seven years was unusually exacting, and when, at his maturity, he was ready to embody in art the inhabitants of what he called "the flat world of the imagination," he was a master craftsman in engraving and etching.

At twenty-five he set up housekeeping in Leicester Square with his wife, Catherine, a gardener's daughter, and by universal acknowledgment, the perfect wife for a man of genius. As a bride, she was illiterate, but Blake taught her to read and write, to copy his manuscripts, color his illuminated books, and even to see visions—no small accomplishment in any wife. She had, as Yeats said, "a love that knew no limit and a friendship that knew no flaw." They lived meagerly in a London flat, sometimes on ten shillings a week, but material surroundings meant little, in the words of Catherine Blake, "to one forever away in Paradise." Whether away in Paradise or at his drawing board, Blake labored day and night, he said, "that enthusiasm and life might not cease." He wrote *Songs of Innocence*, the purest verbal imagery since Shakespeare; composed vast prophecies that nobody read; wrote epics as long as Homer and twenty tragedies as long as *Macbeth*. For bread and butter—and a pot of beer—he depended on illustrations for old and contemporary books—*Job*, *Milton*, *Gray* and *Cowper*—and on his commercial engravings and woodcuts. It was a thin living he got from his endless toil, but he did not expect riches from an art that flouted popular taste, and the rewards that counted most came from his work and the devotion of his wife.

Blake is one of the oddest characters to win immortality in art. With very few exceptions, visionaries are too subjective, or absurd, or stupid to deserve serious consideration; and their formless emissions are those of the nutty girl Huckleberry Finn ran across—the one who couldn't put a proper arm on the figure she was drawing and attached three or four to hide her ineptness—or the infantile trash of the modern expressionists. The Englishman, in half his brain, at least, was almost abnormally lucid and intelligible, and expressed himself in crystalline imagery; but when the psychic stuff bore down upon him, he spun out volumes of theosophical scraps hardly superior, in the aggregate, to the maunderings of table-rappers.

Denouncing most of the great artists of the past, he refused to go directly to nature for his models; in fact, he condemned nature sharply. "A man puts a model before him," he said, "and paints it so neat as to make it a deception. Now I ask any man of sense, is that art? If copying from nature is the art of painting, then it is no better than manual labor; anybody can do it, and fools best of all, as it requires no mind." He put his trust in inspiration and imagination. "Get your imagination going!" he cried. "Work it up till you see the vision, and then you will have the foundation of art!" He had no difficulty in conjuring up the visions, whereupon all sorts of shapes—friends, enemies and animals—were reconstructed and visualized as actual presences. He seemed to recognize these presences when they appeared, as the ordinary man his fellow creatures, and he portrayed them as they trooped before him as "spiritual models." A strange business indeed, and one that squared with nothing advocated by the academies. But the test of art, as the test of anything, lies in the product; and if you are skeptical, you have only to look at Blake's magnificent designs.

Without referring to living models, with stock figures taken from old Renaissance engravings, and Gothic tombs—large-muscled, sexless figures—he created pictures for his own books and for the *Book of Job* and Dante's *Divine Comedy*. An engraver by trade, he believed in the "hard, wiry outline," which he employed to contain his own symbols and to invest inorganic objects with human attributes. His best illustrations, such as those for the *Job*, are as original as anything ever done for a literary text, and in a way, unexampled. He bundled figures together in long rhythmical friezes bending and waving, or in spirals around great trees and oceans and, as likely as not, a screaming God akin to Michelangelo's Deity. His designs are always alive—always full of action; his forms circulate and glide with flying arms and startling recurrences; and they are used to communicate dramatic moods of supplication, almighty wrath, ce-

lestial joy, tenderness, sorrow and terror—the ec-
stasies of the spirit as he embodied them.

Blake engraved, printed, decorated, illuminated
and bound his own books, six artists in one. These
books have been called the most wonderful works
of their kind ever produced, and to those who
have seen them the compliment is not exaggerated.

His philosophy of art, when he put it in verbal
form, was specific enough. With the audacity of
sharp-tempered conviction, he hurled the light-
ning of his visions against the massive corpus of
art erected by the Italians—and fancied he had destroyed it. He believed in inspiration unreservedly
—inspiration as the act of divine revelation—and
denied vehemently the value of referring to the
ordinary business of life for his material. "Nature,"
he screamed, "is the work of the devil! Is it not
reasonable to suppose that one can create, by the
workings of the mind, forms stronger, clearer and
more moving than anything produced by nature?
If not, what is imagination for? And what, in
heaven's name, is the use of art?"

Imagination, passion, inspiration—the terms with
Blake were interchangeable. "Use them actively,
freely, and boldly," he said, "and they will induce
the creative state of mind indispensable to any art
worthy of the name." The opposite condition, he
insisted, was reason, or logic, which he identified
with everything dull, dead, and copied from nature. Better to have evil that is active than good

that is mechanical and sterile. Imagination, or passion, is the sixth sense—the spiritual sense; spirits are organized men; and the body of God is the only reality. Far from curbing our passions, he advocated that we should be mastered by them, taking care, of course, to be mastered by the noblest passions. "When the imagination is inflamed, the vision appears, and when the vision is transcribed by a trained hand, we behold the true divinity of art."

This, needless to say, is mystic doctrine and repugnant to hard-headed realists. We might set against it the dogmas of artists who paint only what the naked eye can see—men like Holbein, Velasquez, and Courbet who said, "Show me an angel and I'll paint it for you." But no good would come of trying to destroy Blake's convictions by the forces arising from observable phenomena. His visions, unlike those of most mystics, happened to be clear-cut, carefully articulated, and bound together by a hard, determinate outline. If you doubt it, you have only to examine his *Job*, or his *Dante*, to be converted. He had no skill at modeling and little knowledge of anatomy, but he triumphed over his deficiencies, and despite his meager equipment, delivered his dreams with amazing certainty and precision.

I F BLAKE refused to have intercourse with nature, his compatriot, Turner, took another road leading to salvation. Turner studied the conformation of the earth with the patience of the scientist and the sensibilities of the artist; and his practical knowledge of natural forms was as comprehensive as Michelangelo's knowledge of the human organism. During his three-score years of incessant artistry, he traveled, mostly on foot, over a large part of the British Isles and western Europe, exploring the structure of the earth, and the heavens above the earth—the antiquity of mountains, the plastic anatomy of the sea, the transitory architecture of the clouds, the course of tides and rivers, the splendor of sunsets and the decay of natural life under the degrading industrialism of man. In the volume of work accomplished, he surpassed all other artists, and every picture that bears his name was done by himself alone.

Turner's life was mysterious and erratic, drifting from early fame and large financial success, to secret debauches and isolated squalor. He was born in ugliness, and the habit of personal slovenliness clung to him like a disease; and as his fame increased, his ambitions expanded proportionately, but to the exclusion of social amenities. Soon he became a recluse who hoarded large sums of money for which he had no use whatever. In common with Michelangelo, he surrendered himself unconditionally to art, and to get the most from his genius, deliberately ignored the conventional obligations which most people assume without complaint, and without thinking.

Joseph Mallord William Turner was born in London, in 1775, the son of a barber. His mother was vicious and ungovernable and her early death was a blessing; his father was windy and greedy, and as the boy rose from rags to riches, he never forgot that he was the son of a barber and was never too proud to keep the barber within range of communication. What made the son an artist and the kind of artist he was, is one of the mysteries of genius. Three minutes from his father's shop ran the great river, the Thames, and as often as he could steal aboard, he rode down to the sea in ships, got the hang of them, and mastered them like a sailor, every rope and spar.

At the age of eleven, he colored engravings at fourpence a plate and in his fourteenth year was admitted to classes in the Royal Academy; at eighteen he was an independent artist with his own studio, and at twenty-seven a full-fledged R.A. The rest of his life he was a famous man—when they could find him. At the Royal Academy, he drew from the nude, and drew very well, and in his early years as an artist, spoke and wrote grammatical English; but as specific needs arose, he became the solitary painter of landscape and the sea, and as such, discarded the nude and the formalities of English. In the course of time, his syntax and spelling were those of a rustic.

From fifteen to twenty-five, Turner made topographical studies of country estates—careful drawings done to order as wall decorations for the owners; and roaming about England, conquered the new art of transparent water colors which he made peculiarly his own. He was a born tramp, walking twenty-five miles a day, capable of sleeping anywhere and eating anything, and working day after day, rain or shine. If no water was handy, he spat into his powdered colors and made pictures of magical purity. He loved the land, but the sea even more, and lashed to the mast, sailed the British coastline in heavy gales so that he might observe the structure of the waves and the shifting contours of the clouds.

At twenty-five, Turner began to live with his housekeeper, a girl of sixteen, and the menage continued to his death, the girl protecting his paintings and his seclusion, while he wandered over the Continent from Venice to France, studying the manifestations of nature. It is not certain that he loved his housekeeper, or anyone else; for his physical urgencies were requited by low-grade intrigues which netted him four illegitimates whom he disowned. With advancing age and overmuch painting, he drank immoderately and spent his week ends in carnal dissipations in the dives of the East End.

In his last years, he was an old hermit buried in paint. His imagination was disorganized by dirt and hard liquor; and his house—originally an imposing affair with huge galleries for his paintings—was a ruin. The rains beat in; the rats fattened, and the great works of art for which he sacrificed his life disintegrated in the accumulating debris. A little off the beam, he left his faithful housekeeper and bunked with a cancerous old crone in Chelsea near the river. Known to the marine ruck as "The Admiral" from his habit of observing the weather conditions, he died before his rendezvous was discovered.

Turner's models were not human beings, whom he regarded with suspicion, nor the performances of human beings which, to him, ended in desecration, but the phenomena of the world of nature as it stood uncontaminated by the foul inventiveness of man. He was no polite amateur copying the pleasing aspects of nature, but a probing, analytical student who searched the face of nature as rigorously as Holbein searched the face of an English lord. Days on end he watched the tides and the erosive action of moving waters; years on end he

charted the stratification of the earth as it had been
formed under the pressure of sedimentary deposits
and the mountainous upheavals with their igneous
outcroppings; and for at least two decades he
delved into the effects of light and atmosphere—
with the result that a group of French artists, in a
round-robin epistle, hailed him as the father of impressionism. He made thousands and tens of thousands of drawings and two thousand finished pictures to prove his emotions of delight and wonder,
and conversely, his sadness and despair. Nature always, and then man against nature—such was the
burden of his art!

In his younger days, he used his models more
or less realistically from sustained observation: wit-
ness *Calais Pier* and *The Shipwreck*, perhaps the
most rugged and exciting—and truthful—accounts
of ships and the sea ever recorded in paint. He
could paint a water color of a full-rigged ship
speeding before a gale in three hours—literal
enough to satisfy an old salt and dramatic enough
to delight a connoisseur. The realistic mood
yielded to enormous, riotous fantasies—Old Testament melodramas and mythological conceptions
in which his knowledge of maritime life was sub-
limated into Homeric dreams. First, the founda-
tions—the solid earth, the sculptured sea endlessly
rocking, the ships and squalls and the waves pil-
ing up like masonry—the sea as it rocks in the minds
of old sailors and old poets. Modern industrialism

he hated, but notwithstanding, from a Great Western Express train as a model, he painted *Rain, Steam and Speed*, the most enchanting picture to come out of the developments of modern science.

Having wrestled with nature for half a century, he tried in his old age to transcend nature as Shakespeare did in *The Tempest*, and to create miracles of light and atmosphere. The real, or everyday world, was dissolved, like some unsubstantial pageant faded; the Yorkshire hills reared themselves as sunlit mountains, and the Thames became a river of light. Nothing remained but dramatic illumination: white light and scarlet shadow; the sun bathing a wreck of ships sinking in a veil of blood and fire, in a radiance of gold and white, or scarlet and emerald.

No artist, of course, can preserve his youthful enthusiasm for living models and living tissue. In the end Michelangelo dismissed his athletes and relied on formulas; and Goya, shutting his doors against the women who haunted him, produced monsters. Turner, after fifty years of devotion to land and sea, suffered an artist's ascension. Forsaking his loyal housekeeper for a diseased old woman, he lifted himself, imaginatively, into the seventh heaven, where his models were radiance and light, and the splendor twice removed from the sordid stuff of human relations. The story is that the sun shone upon his face as he died.

John James Audubon, one of the major glories of American art and literature, has become a national hero and a legendary figure beloved alike by conservationists of wildlife and confused young painters seeking inspiration in examples of pioneer fortitude. While he lived, it was a different story, and his struggles to complete a great work in the face of poverty and opposition have an epic quality about them, notwithstanding the vanity of the man, his unreasonable suspicions, and his inability to credit rivals with honorable intentions.

Audubon himself, by reason of a tricky memory and also by his flair for the dramatic, is largely responsible for the myths attached to his name, and to this day, not all the facts of his life have been definitely separated from the handmade legends. He gave it out that he came from New Orleans of exalted lineage, but recently it has come to light that he was born in Santo Domingo, in 1785, the illegitimate son of a French naval officer and a nameless Creole mistress. It is certain that he began to draw in his childhood and concurrently manifested an interest in birds which, before his arrival at manhood, developed into an absorbing passion and a profession. Captain Audubon, the father, encouraged his talents, and on his return to France gave his son the education of a young aristocrat: more drawing, fencing, shooting, and English.

Jean Jacques, as he was called in France, was sent to a military school which he deserted when his studies in art and nature were curtailed; and his father, unperturbed, enrolled him in the classes of David, the dictator of French art and official painter successively for the Kingdom, Republic, Terror, Directory and Empire. It is not probable that the young naturalist learned much from David whose paintings, portraits excepted, were concocted by rigid and ridiculous academic laws, but his cast drawing at least had the virtue of driving him to more perceptive ornithological investigations.

In 1803, Captain Audubon emigrated to America and chose, as his temporary home, an estate near Philadelphia, in which city his son, now John James, fell in love with a beautiful girl. To prove his competence as a provider—a stipulation of the girl's father—young Audubon worked, for five years, as a clerk in an importing house in New York. It was tough going for a proud, sensitive, handsome, ambitious youth, but John J. was not one to acknowledge discouragement. In 1813 he married the girl and took her, on their honeymoon, down the Ohio on a flatboat to Louisville, a perilous voyage in those days, but of inestimable value to the career of the groom who began, at firsthand, to make the studies of wildlife on which his fame solidly rests. In Kentucky he opened a trader's exchange which netted him only a little; and met the Scottish naturalist, Alexander Wilson, who was peddling subscriptions to a book on American birds. With ruffled vanity and a resentment strange in a man of his parts, Audubon never had a good word for Wilson and charged him, on no grounds whatever, of plagiarism.

The exchange folded, and also his grist-mill, and Audubon, with his wife and son, took a boat for New Orleans. On the voyage he made more drawings of wildlife. In New Orleans the family lived close to starvation, saved by the artist's portrait commissions and his wife's pittance as a teacher. Returning to Philadelphia, the ambitious painter studied with Sully—an odd choice, Sully being a maker of conventional likenesses—and solicited subscriptions to his projected volume, the elephant folio of *The Birds of America*. From paintings in water color, he published in London from 1827 to 1838 the great edition of the work, 435 hand-colored impressions from aquatint engravings, the most remarkable book of its kind in existence. Today, few copies of the original folio remain intact, most of them having been unbound and dispersed as single prints, for extraordinary sums.

In the literary circles of Europe, Audubon, who

had carried a silver dagger in the wilderness, displayed his talent for self-dramatization by wearing long hair and posing as an esthetic Leatherstocking. His last years were spent happily with his children and grandchildren on an estate above the Hudson River, near New York. As the "Sage of Morningside Heights," he was an international possession, and before his death in 1851, Audubon Societies were springing up at home and abroad.

Audubon is the only artist whose pictures of birds rank with the masterpieces in other branches of painting. His eminence in his particular field has never been seriously threatened, and his most sedulous followers, by comparison, are little better than taxidermists in paint. It is doubtless true, to a degree, that the qualities which made him outstanding as a bird-painter, might have brought him equal distinction in other subject matter. His portraits of men and women are certainly distinguished, far better in fact than the efforts of most of our practitioners, but they are not in the same class as his portraits of birds. It is here that the old question of the model enters the picture, and the artist, like everybody else, does his best work when his strongest interests are involved. His portraits of human beings are excellent, but his birds are unique—immeasurably more alive and impressive.

Audubon's water colors of birds are ornithologically accurate and scientifically useful, but their significance as art springs from the imagination of the artist and the effective accentuations he made without falsifying his material. He explored the swamps of Louisiana, the forests of Ohio, and the coastline of the Carolinas, with the convictions of the early Jesuits—a man with a mission, actuated by a religious zeal to preserve forever, in graphic form, the feathered life of America.

He had an eye for dramatic situations and a startling originality of design which, in each case, was determined by the individuality and habitat of his models. He sketched his wild models from life and painted them at leisure, entrusting the local color and landscape to assistants. Dull birds at rest could not excite him—he must catch them in instants of suspense or fright. Thus, when he painted hawks—and he painted all kinds of hawks—he presented them in predacious attitudes, killing their prey, flying off with a fish in their talons, or tearing at the entrails of a duck.

Again and again, Audubon introduced into his pictures of some birds a messenger of terror and death in the shape of a rattlesnake. His huge golden eagle soars aloft carrying a live rabbit; some of his birds are caught in the act of mating, and his large stately specimens—his wild turkeys, cranes and herons—have more personality than the portraits of average human beings. Audubon's birds are humanized, and it may be said that no painter testifies more eloquently to the importance of the model—

the natural, unforced preoccupation with subjects which releases creative energy.

Audubon is eternal proof of the precept first advanced by an old Italian architect who said, "Nature produces the material but genius produces the form." The material provided by nature is unlimited in variety and quantity, open to every artist for the taking, and often exciting in its own right. It may be pleasing and consoling in its organic state, but no photograph can raise nature into the realm of art for the simple reason that the camera has no soul, no personality, and no mind.

The above comment was prompted by a recent examination of the followers of Audubon, both the imitators and those artists who claim to have more scientific knowledge of bird life than was granted the Franco-American master. The trouble with the scientific artists is that they ape nature too sedulously, and in the end succeed only in giving us photographs of a bird; and the trouble with imitators is that they copy Audubon instead of nature and produce something less worthy than photography. Without departing seriously from scientific truth, Audubon, by using his imagination, his infallible sense of the dramatic, and his originality as a designer, created a kingdom of art that will remain his own for a long time.

HOGARTH

Lord Lovat

Plate 17

Keelmen Heaving in Coals by Moonlight

Plate 18

Plate 19

BLAKE
The Morning Stars Sang Together

Plate 20

Two Lawyers

Le Déjeuner sur l'Herbe

Plate 21

Blue Corn

Plate 22

TOULOUSE-LAUTREC
La Goulue

Plate 23

Plate 24

JOHN JAMES AUDUBON
Snowy Heron

Honoré Daumier was born in Marseilles in 1808 and came to Paris as a child when his father, an excellent glazier but a mediocre poet, hoped vaguely to gain recognition in the world of letters. The recognition was denied him and the Daumiers, desperately poor, allowed their son to take his destiny in his own hands and make what he could of it. There was no need to lie awake at night worrying about the boy: he was sure of himself from his seventh year and his life, though hard and materially less profitable than a hod carrier's, was artistically rich and satisfactory. Honoré began to draw before he learned the secrets of the streets, and hating formal training, had the best education open to a boy of his resolution —the gutter. He grew up in the streets, and to mitigate the sting of poverty, roamed the Louvre, looking at pictures. In middle-age, a famous man, he made a lithograph of a party of visitors in the big museum of art: two pedagogues shepherding groups of helpless children. One says to the other: "You take yours on this side, and I'll do the other and we'll finish the room in a jiffy."

Nobody told him what pictures to admire; nobody tried to impress him with a little learning. He was on his own, and naturally, was attracted to the works of art containing something of himself—to Rembrandt who binds together all unfortunate souls and to the sculptures of Michelangelo for there was, as Balzac pointed out, "much of Michelangelo in the boy." The art student from the gutter made sketches in emulation of his favorites, and from the sketches, little modelings in clay or wax which hinted of the power to come.

For a time he was an usher at court, which meant that he wore a black gown and conducted idlers to their seats to watch the behavior of the law. Next, he was a bookseller's drudge and after that a professional artist. Before he was twenty he had somehow mastered lithography and had published in this medium a series of pictures which, for draftsmanship and characterization, are unexcelled in French art. His work caught the eye of the editor of a radical sheet, and he joined the staff, at twenty-one, on the promise of unlimited freedom. In a few months, the unterrified gamin, turning his heavy artillery on the Orleans politicians, had won unenviable notoriety, and each week, when his cartoon appeared, ministers of state shook in their boots. After taking a shot at Louis Philippe, Daumier was locked up, but he bore his sentence cheerfully and on his release, proceeded in exactly the same direction. His paper folded and he went to another, and to his death, earned his bread by cartooning.

He lived in an old house on the Quai d'Anjou in the most ancient quarter of the city with his wife, Marie, a seamstress. In 1848, the year of his marriage, he began to paint in oils and his canvases, though rejected by official juries, won the admiration of the best men in Paris. He derived no money from his oils and to keep alive depended on his lithographs, sometimes slaving at eight stones simultaneously to earn a brief interlude for painting. At the end of the day, sitting by his window above the Seine, he would fix his tired eyes on the boats, the fishermen, the laundresses and poor mothers scrubbing children, and he would remark to himself, "I have my art to comfort me, but what have these wretched men and women to live for?"

His friends were the celebrities of Paris—Delacroix, Courbet, Baudelaire, and Gautier—but he did not seek them. They assembled in his humble quarters in the spirit of homage, sat on the floor because there were no chairs, smoked and drank beer together. They knew who was the great man among them. One night, while Daumier was busy with his lithographs, a remark was passed. "Isn't it too bad," the speaker asked, "that old Daumier has to work for a living?" Overhearing the comment, Daumier turned, straightened up, and with a toss of his magnificent head, replied very slowly, underlining each word. "It isn't too bad that I have to work," he said. "The trouble is that I have to work too hard, for my eyes are getting pretty bad. But I must remind you kind-hearted gentlemen of something: you have an income—but I have a public. And I'll take the public."

He retired to a cottage in the country to ease his vision, and eked out a bare subsistence by social or humorous cartoons for which glib editors wrote captions. Facing eviction, he was saved by Corot who bought the house and deeded it over to his friend with best wishes, as a birthday remembrance. In his last years, he was offered the ribbon of the Legion of Honor, which he refused quietly, not blatantly as Courbet advised him to do, in the interest of publicity. A loan exhibition of his works in color and black-and-white, held in 1878, did not pay gallery expenses, and the following year, he died, blind and paralytic, and was buried by the state.

Daumier brought his great work to the completion before the hocus-pocus of modernism and the exploitation of claptrap had alienated art from humanity. In some respects he was unique among Frenchmen; he hired no models to pose for him, no bored females to undress and stand fatuously in a corner while he copied the texture of their skins and the high lights on their protuberances. "The people of Paris going about their business are my models," he said; and he studied their occupational attitudes; dug into their battered souls; observed the lines and planes that hardships had written in their faces and the sculptural twist of their bodies as they washed clothes or swept the streets. His subject matter was gathered from the universal aspects of French life, the elemental things that Rembrandt, before him, had loved and painted. He delineated what he had seen at firsthand, and he painted with a depth of feeling conspicuously missing in French art.

For example, let us look at one of his most cherished models, the lawyer. As an usher in the courts, he had watched the lawyers perform, and had said, "There is nothing in the world more fascinating than the mouth of a lawyer in operation." He had seen shysters puffing out hypocritical arguments in the defense of crooks and felons, making justice a snide thing; and after recording his observations in caricatures of wax, had hurried to his garret to amplify them in lithography. As his art matured, he put the lawyers in his magazine cartoons and in his independent studies; and no other artist, past or present, has drawn the human mouth with such incisiveness, mobility, and awesome strength. A surgeon or anatomist could not fashion these mouths if he dissected a thousand mandibles, and no artist could achieve such plasticity if he copied the faces of all the lawyers in Christendom—unless he were blessed with Daumier's convictions about the pleaders. The lawyer did something to Daumier's soul and he, reciprocating, did something to them, and the interaction, combined with years of technical knowledge, produced the work of art, the created lawyer who is indisputably a Daumier job.

All told, some 4,500 lithographs carry the initials H.D.; prints that have set the high-water mark for all subsequent workers on stone—and you can still buy them for a few dollars. Daumier's oils are few and far between, but intrinsically and in terms of the market, almost beyond price. One of the best, *The Third-class Railway Carriage* at the Metropolitan Museum, and one of several versions of the subject, is about as profound a painting as the world has seen in the last hundred years. It represents his models going about their daily business: three seats in a compartment, with two women in the first, one suckling a baby, the other, very old with a sleeping boy at her side; and in the background rows of passengers, some full-face, some in profile, several in back view. Here are models habitually considered and pondered over, filled with pity and magnanimity, with the human substance poured into them by a great soul; here in plain faces and bodies as solid as clay, we have the story of the dreariness of one aspect of French life, and the portraits of God's creatures fashioned of the stuff that endures forever.

IN THE ELEGANCE of Èdouard Manet is centered for the first time and to perfection, the distinction which the French have brought to modern painting. Manet was a Parisian of the old school, a man of cultivation and a man of the world, loyal to his friends and to his principles and within the limits of his own conception of painting, one of the best men of the nineteenth century. He was born in 1832, of moneyed parents who frowned on art as a profession, and to cure their obdurate son of his esthetic propensities sent him down to Rio as a merchant mariner. The voyage, however, only strengthened his pertinacity, and on his return he studied with an old academic fogy named Couture whom he shocked by his experiments in realistic subject matter. Repudiating the salon-master, he spent much of his time in the Louvre and fell in love with the Spaniards. In the evenings, he took piano lessons from a young woman who became his mistress, the mother of his son, and in the course of events, his lawfully wedded wife.

A brilliant technician, he opened his own studio in 1860, and two years later, at the death of his father, came into a competency. His exhibitions in 1863-64 brought down upon him the ignorant and frenzied denunciations of hidebound critics and sham-classic painters, who had also lived with mistresses but had refused to marry them. They fell foul upon Manet and in the vocabulary of deranged guttersnipes called him everything he was not—a sensation-monger, a notoriety-hound, a carnal exhibitionist, and a merchant of pruriency. Civilized Frenchmen like Baudelaire, Gautier and Zola rallied to his defense, but the mischief had been done and Manet, a sensitive soul, never recovered from the wounds inflicted by his fool detractors. To soothe his nerves, he went to Spain to study Goya; and returned to his Parisian studio as one of the leaders of a revolt derisively labeled impressionism. There was no market for his pictures and suffering from the protracted abuse, he became something of a paranoiac, and died a nervous wreck in his fiftieth year.

Influenced by Velasquez, he accepted painting as a job to be done, but the variety of his interests far exceeded that of the cloistered Spaniard. No Bohemian dilettante, he took his occupation very seriously, and trained his superlative workmanship on subjects taken from the bull ring, the racecourse, and the bar of the Folies Bergères, to portraits of models of high and low degree. He brought into the dull officialdom of his time the quality of unexpectedness, the freshness of vivid impressions and of things seen clearly in radiant light and artful patterns. He discovered new and exciting arrangements of tones and painted with a caressing elegance that left its mark on Whistler and two generations of students.

The French, I am sorry to say, were horrified, and two of his paintings precipitated the crisis. The trouble arose in 1863 when he met a red-headed girl named Victorine Meurend in the lobby of a public building. She was not beautiful but she had the macabre dwarfish charm of one of Baudelaire's demivirgins and he took her to his studio and made her the sole model of his house and heart. Manet painted Victorine again and again: in straight portraits and in costume as a matador, a dancer, or one of those old women who keep harlots. The picture that ruined his reputation was called *Luncheon on the Grass*, a scene representing Victorine in the nude, with a companion grisette also unclothed, at an alfresco repast in the company of two fully dressed gentlemen—a modernization of an old Venetian theme. The French people, not more conventional than most of us, shivered for the safety of their shopgirls.

Two years later, Manet exhibited *Olympia*, a landmark in the history of hypocritical indignation. Again the model was the redhead, this time, half-recumbent on a bed, her pale, bluish-white nakedness guarded by a Negress bearing flowers and a black cat sniffing at her feet. The picture was rejected by the Salon amid howls that sent old lechers from their kept girls back into the sanctity of their homes, and thirty years were to elapse before the *Olympia* found an appropriate home in the Louvre.

The French, you see, were not ready for Manet's honesty with his models and with his art. They approved, of course, of nudes and harlots; but for the sake of their culture and the trumped-up glory of La Patrie, they demanded something less ingenuous than Manet's Victorine—a classical goddess, or a charming bit of merchandise disguised as a nymph or the pagan daughter of an old deity.

For his honesty, the artist paid the penalty of persecution. He painted other models, Spanish dancers and demimondaines who came to his studio in the French spirit of conviviality, but when he asked the same freedom accorded to the old painters like Titian and Rubens, he was branded for life. At the present time, Manet's art, notwithstanding its technical excellence and its objectivity, is not in very great demand. His theories about the relative unimportance of subject matter have been carried into a world of pure abstractions in which his elegance is regarded as old-fashioned.

Henri de Toulouse-Lautrec, born at Albi in southern France in 1864, is the only simon-pure aristocrat to win top-flight honors in the republic of art. His father, Count Alphonse de Toulouse-Lautrec-Monfa, was an eccentric blue blood who traced his ancestry in direct line to the noblest families of the thirteenth century, and his mother, of equally long name, was a lady of blood and quality. Both were above honest toil, and being landed patricians at Albi and Bordeaux, lived in the style and cultivated arrogance which the world of today would never countenance. It is not uncommon for aristocrats to patronize the arts, and to surround themselves with objects of art, but when they breed an honest-to-God artist, they really make atonement for their centuries of futility.

The old Count of Toulouse, the sire, was a character out of the past, and his son Henri ran true to form, to an extent: he inherited his father's love of horses and outdoor sports, but a couple of accidents removed him from the rôle of participant to that of artist-spectator. Suffering from some strange infirmity of the bones, he twice stumbled and fell in his childhood, breaking both thighs, and the best the doctors could do was to save him but to leave him crippled for life. His torso developed normally but his legs shriveled into the underpinning of a dwarf and if art had not claimed him, his proud father would have secreted him in the tall towers of a castle in Bordeaux.

In his teens, when the highborn cripple painted horses and wild animals, and took them more or less literally, his father was well pleased; but later, in Paris, when the gifted son's art flowered in the dirt, and his subjects were selected from the half-world, the old aristocrat was furious. At the age of twenty-three, by arrangement with his family, Lautrec came into a private income and a studio of his own in Montmartre, next door to a crusty celibate named Degas, whose relations with his models were anything but orthodox.

In such surroundings, one of the rarest things in art occurred. The young painter named Toulouse-Lautrec, son of Count Alphonse, et cetera, physically deformed but mentally superior to his colleagues—and to the cabinet officers of France—and courted by the aristocrats of Paris, deliberately cast his lot with the lowest forms of life—the specialists in sin and perversity. As naturally as a duck to water, he found his way to the music halls, the one-ring circuses, low-down "dancings," brothels and dives of the underworld. His companion on these noctambulant forays was his mother's cousin, a tall, lean, doctor of medicine, and a quainter pair of birds could not be imagined. The two atavists were hand in glove: the doctor took the artist to the hospitals where Lautrec sketched clinical operations, and by way of recompense, the artist convoyed a bevy of girls from Montmarte to the hospitals for the edification of the patients, just as movie stars in the late war shook their shapely thighs for the delight of wounded G.I.'s.

Lautrec was at his peak from twenty-eight to thirty, during which time he produced his incomparable posters, oils and lithographs of Montmartre, and the nether world of jockeys, pimps, cancan dancers, Lesbians and talented degenerates. His second home was the Moulin Rouge, and his third the *maisons closes,* or houses of prostitution. He was at ease among the whores and would live with them, collectively, for a fortnight at a time; and with no false modesty they would reveal to him naturally, as in the line of duty, one might say, the unaccountable ways of men who segregate certain obliging females for the purposes of carnal satisfaction. He would carry the girls with him to the race-courses for a whiff of fresh air and on excursion boats, and the girls, not unreasonably, adored him. They loved him, not as a well-heeled philanthropist but as the descendant of blue bloods, and one and all, if he had given them the nod, would have made the bed to him.

A life of this stamp, with its febrile activities, its drinking, debaucheries and hard work—for Lautrec was a tireless worker—would have slain a whole man, much less a dwarf, and the artist was clapped into an asylum for dipsomania. His father, disgusted with the turn of events, said bluntly, "Send Henri to England where the lords get drunk every day." During his therapeutic incarceration, Henri executed about fifty drawings, and on the day of his emancipation, rehabilitated and bristling with ideas, crossed the Channel to attend the trial of Oscar Wilde. He made a decorative sketch of Oscar, the bloated Prince of the Black Irises, and returned to France where he lined his portfolio with pictures called *Elles*, or young fillies at their toilet; and he made a good living from his posters and illustrations—though he had no need to work for a living. He invented the poster as it is known today, and made it a work of art, and none of his successors has remotely rivaled him as a portrait-designer.

Lautrec went to Havre, in 1889, to pay his ancestral respects to a lovely English barmaid he had met years before—he made a painting of the "English" and she was a beauty—but the girl had fled with a tout; and sensible of his dwindling powers, he hurried to his mother in Bordeaux. He died there at the age of thirty-six, and the splendor of the noblemen of Toulouse was buried with him.

Toulouse-Lautrec was one of the finest French

draftsman of the nineteenth century. If literary comparisons are valid, he resembled de Maupassant: each, in his own medium, was harsh, honest, and totally devoid of sentimentality, and each interpreted French manners courageously. Lautrec did not employ his actors as isolated models, but as human characters springing from and affected by their environment.

His models, apart from a few portraits of illustrious connections, were the citizens of a degraded world. He respected them and one and all would be dead and forgotten but for his paintings and posters. His favorite model was Jane Avril, a dancer of the Moulin Rouge, a thin-flanked acrobatic girl whom he took with him on his jaunts about Paris—to the hypocritical horror of the aristocrats —and whose exotic graces never failed to inspire him. Another dancer set him to work, La Goulue, a tough, hawk-faced wench who, when her legs failed her, became a lion tamer in a cheap circus. The panels which Lautrec painted for her caravans are now in the Louvre.

One of the singers at the Moulin Rouge rose to fame overnight. She was very young, pale, and slender, with the breasts of a boy and the chaste, credulous eyes of a child. Her name was Yvette Guilbert and her songs were lewd and witty. Growing older and more sensitive, with a mop of orange hair and an amazingly expressive but unlovely face, she was afraid of Lautrec's brush, but he won her over and put her into his best posters, which is to say, the best posters ever made.

The lees of Bohemia—the cultivated daughters of evil, the sisters of Satan, the pimps and patrons, the *fin de siècle* world which, more likely than not, is gone forever, as an actuality—such was Lautrec's field and he adorned it with all the persuasiveness of his art.

He included in his immortal gallery of posters, Aristide Bruant, the first of the performing apaches; "Chocolat," the Negro dancer; Cleo de Merode, whose serpentine belly dance captivated Anatole France; and Loie Fuller, the Illinois farm girl who was taken seriously as an esthetic pioneer because of her spectacular effects obtained by incandescent lighting. And when the debasing world of Montmartre amusements palled on him, Lautrec retreated, for a week or two, into the houses of prostitution where he was a welcome guest. The girls went about their unaccountable business while he sketched them, or off duty, gathered around him as a complimentary gesture to his affectionate concern. One of his paintings of the reception room of a bordello, with the various types of merchandise sitting at attention, says about everything that can be said of the selling of flesh.

Van Gogh is the modern incarnation of the Biblical truth that by faith you shall be made whole, and of the old esthetic truth that an ounce of conviction is worth a ton of talent. The cards seemed to be stacked against this ugly Dutchman from the outset, but in the end he triumphed—to become one of the most original and appealing of latter-day painters. Outwardly, he was something to make children run and hide; candid and holy to the few who learned to know him, and to others, a composite of peasant, convict and Christian martyr. He had a mattoid cranium and cropped red hair, a large nose, a snapping mouth that worked like a trap, and deep-sunken, green eyes that stared at the world with the unblinking innocence of an infant, or the ghastly prescience of an inspired fanatic.

Vincent Van Gogh, a preacher's son, was born in Holland, in 1853, and would gladly have entered the church himself, had he been more personable and articulate. In the autumn of 1869, he was sent to the Hague to work in the branch office of the famous Goupils, of Paris, dealers in art. He entered upon his duties with the same enthusiasm that impelled him to a literal acceptance of Christianity, and in his twentieth year was promoted to the London branch of the firm.

He did well in London—wore a frock coat and a topper and smoked his pipe contentedly until he fell in love with his landlady's daughter, Ursula. Sensitive and forbidding, he needed and sought a woman's love, but every move he made in that direction was cruelly repulsed. He worshipped the ground Ursula walked on, but she spurned his proposals and her mocking laughter nearly killed him. By the merciful intervention of his superiors, he was transferred to the home office of Goupils, in Paris.

Here, the young zealot talked religion, instead of pictures, to the gallery's sophisticated clientele, made a nuisance of himself, and departed suddenly to London to test his Christianity in the rôle of lay evangelist in the slums. His duties brought him in contact with the lowest of mortals, and for reasons known only to his Maker, he began to make sketches of his surroundings. His first efforts were crude but promising, and when his brother, Theo, an art dealer in Paris, saw them, he was delighted beyond words. But some years were to elapse before art finally claimed Vincent as her saint—and her slave.

Repulsed the second time by Ursula, he buried himself among the miners of Belgium as an unordained minister of the Gospel, and the miners opened their hearts to him for he was one of them, teaching children to read, taking care of the sick and comforting the aged and infirm. His drawings of the coal diggers, though poorly constructed, indicated a faith that could move mountains and a voice that, sooner or later, humanity would hear. "I am trying to save my soul," Vincent wrote to Theo, "and I work in living flesh and blood, as Christ did, the greatest of artists."

He yearned for a woman's love, but no woman smiled on him, and he wandered into Holland and back to Paris and then home again, suffering always and drawing when he could find time. In Antwerp he fell in love with a prostitute who consented to be his model, a pock-marked, pregnant tramp in the last stages of drunkenness. He made a drawing of her and called it *Sorrow*, and beneath it inscribed the words, "How is it that a woman could be so alone and so deserted?" He consorted with the ill-famed creature until Theo arrived from Paris to reclaim him, ragged, half-starved and on the verge of prostration.

"I am no good," Vincent remarked, "but I feel the humanity in all of us."

He returned to Holland; fell in love again, but to no purpose; and painted *The Potato Eaters*, a sooty picture of peasants at table, but indicative of the originality that lay deep within his tortured soul. Only a few years remained to him and he made use of them like a doomed man awaiting the executioner.

In need of technical training he enrolled in an art school at Antwerp where he was nothing short of a riot, with his queer face and appalling candor. He painted a thin model as he desired her to be—with an ample belly and massive haunches; and when asked to pare her down, shouted defiantly, "A woman should have a pelvis that can support a child."

In Paris, attended by his brother, his sole means of subsistence, he studied at Montmartre with the impressionists—Pissarro, Lautrec and Seurat—who recognized his ability and encouraged him. His days were numbered and he hurried to the South of France to make his peace with the world that was killing him. He rented, thanks to Theo, a little house in Arles—the House of Light he called it—and in three frenzied years painted most of the canvases upon which his fame stands today. "I must start all over again," he said, "get down to earth, feel the warmth of the sun and smell the ploughed fields."

Fearlessly, he tackled the job—his mission in the world—and painted like an inspired maniac; painted hatless in the sun, hundreds of pictures, each one at a single sitting. "How wonderful the sun!" he shrieked. "And my yellow house of light!" It was like a dream come true, until a cynical killjoy named Gauguin came down from Paris to share the house, and to drive Vincent to madness and desperation. Gauguin sneered at his pictures, and to mortify him, took him to a local brothel to make merry with the girls. Vincent was not a whoremaster; he was serious with the wheedling inmates, and when one of them, a heartless brunette, double-crossed him and asked him as a joke for one of his ears as a Christmas gift, he returned to his house, half-crazed, to think it over. His mind unhinged, he cut off his right ear with a razor and despatched it by the brothel porter to the unconscionable bitch who had played upon his credulity.

The end was around the corner. His brother sent him to the hospital and when the wound was mended, to a private asylum at Auvers, near Paris. Unbalanced at intervals, profoundly lucid at times, he painted the landscape around him and the doctors assigned to him. One day, he saw everything clearly, as if by a stroke of revelation, and there was no hope. He saw himself permanently mad, and calmly fired a bullet into his stomach. "I have been shooting," he said gently to those who found him, and after a final puffing at his old pipe, he died at the age of thirty-seven. They buried him in the cornfield he had loved to paint.

Van Gogh had the right idea. He wanted to make pictures for the world, for everybody—to make people listen to him as they listened to Shakespeare and Dickens and Mark Twain—to make pictures, he said "for women rocking cradles and sailors on the high seas." Tragically the odds were against him. Spasmodically trained and at times off his base, he painted like one possessed to compensate for his irregular youth. Despite his limitations, he shines out today as one of the most fascinating of modern artists, one of the few in truth, whose notions of painting will bear analysis. He painted straight from nature and straight from the depths of his soul, and his pictures are symbols of his convulsive wretchedness, the collision of an abnormally responsive organism with the over-powering stimuli of light, color and humanity.

In the throes of an ecstatic mood, he worked with unnatural rapidity, and the models which, to most artists, are only routine subjects, transported him out of this world. A pair of old shoes, a bunch of sunflowers, a cornfield with crows flying above it, inflamed his imagination as the primitive paint-ers were inflamed by the Nativity or Crucifixion; and in his haste to preserve the mood, he applied his paint in streaks, like molten lava, in smiting colors of yellow and blue and in a personal style that is remarkably effective, despite the crudities of draftsmanship. He loved to paint the lowly and uncritical: beggars, and babies in long dresses, and old women "with faces," he said, "like dusty blades of grass," and "young girls as fresh as the fields, every line of them virgin."

Vincent, as he naïvely signed his paintings, left his mark on modern art in still life and portraiture, and when he was in a lunatic asylum, in landscapes which, he explained, "call forth the feeling of fright and wonder." His models were the human beings and landscapes contemplated through his wild green eyes: himself, at his easel or smoking his pipe; blazing sunflowers, yellow against yellow, the color he associated with eternity; the old color man, in Paris, who sold him his pigments, and the old haunts in Montmartre where he worked with the impressionists.

The town of Arles was his model, with his little house and his bedroom, the town billiard hall where he tried to fraternize with local sports who brushed him off, and the brothel that cost him an ear and his reason. One of his masterpieces is a portrait of his old landlady; another, the bearded postman of Arles, Roulin, who brought the money orders from Theo, and Roulin's wife and grown-up son. He painted tall cypress trees in the moonlight, and during his incarceration at Auvers, the most fearsome and agitated landscapes of recent times. Every artist, of course, paints himself, no matter how objective he may be; and Van Gogh's last things are examples of what happens to the model when the artist is on the border-line of reason. He saw the calm earth in a state of convulsion, the fields hurtling in agony, the houses lurching toward an awful and dramatic sky—everything as a reflection of the inner turmoil and the conviction that carried him forward in his art and carried him to his doom.

Van Gogh is exceptionally free from the nonsensical dreams and moronic sentiments characteristic of unbalanced minds held captive by art. Sometimes, in the heat of a terrible passion, he deformed nature into a seething organism that has no meaning to most of us—but he never brought forth a platitude.

In calmer moods, when the spasm of paint had passed, Van Gogh was capable of profound reflections on art. He believed with Tolstoy and Dickens that art should have a purpose—a message, if you will—not exactly the burden of a moral code but a meaning that should be accepted as a spiritual necessity; that it should act as a true religion to bring social groups together and make the world a better place for everybody. A humble man—one acquainted with the lowest orders of society—he tried to make paintings for the uneducated emotions—for peasants and manual laborers and sailors. By the irony of fate, his paintings, every last one of them, have become objects of speculation traveling from auction rooms to wealthy collectors and museums. None but the favored few can afford a Van Gogh, but whenever a representative collection of his pictures is brought before the public, multitudes come from far and near to marvel at the naked, blinding humanity of his tortured conceptions.

Plate 25

CÉZANNE
Apples and Primroses
(DETAIL)

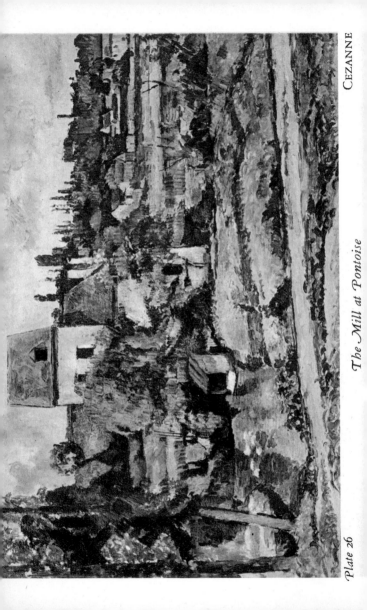

Plate 26

The Mill at Pontoise

CEZANNE

Plate 27

Both Members of This Club

GEORGE BELLOWS

Plate 28

GRANT WOOD
American Gothic

Plate 29

JOHN STEUART CURRY
The Line Storm

Plate 30

THOMAS HART BENTON
The Music Lesson

To my friend Th. Craven
Reginald Marsh

REGINALD MARSH
Two Girls

Plate 31

Plate 32

Promenade

Charles Burchfield

IN 1861, a young provincial of twenty-two came up to Paris from the South of France to try his luck among the smart practitioners of painting. His name was Paul Cézanne and he was not precisely equipped to compete with the boys of the capital, being inhibited, boorish, unpersonable, poorly trained and as obstinate as a mule. But he was no fool; nor was he wanting in courage, patience and good judgment of the leading artists of the day. Thin-skinned and morbidly shy, he disguised his apprehensions by unpredictable outbursts of temper, and by affecting a Bohemian swagger that relieved the yokel in him. He was a problem painter, no doubt about that, and his best friends were embarrassed by his antics, but fortunately, his father was a rich banker, and he could afford the luxury of his high ideals.

The conventional asses presiding over the *Beaux Arts* rejected his application insolently, and for ten years he worked more or less alone, without appearing to get anywhere. He was a colorist by the grace of God and he was never trivial; but when he tried to rival clever men like Delacroix, Courbet and Manet, his failures were monumental. When the jury of the official Salon turned him down cold, he was cut to the quick and belligerently petitioned the unfeeling wretches to reconsider their decision. His heartbreaking experiences in Paris were counterbalanced by his annual return to the South where he could paint landscapes without fear of ridicule.

At twenty-eight, Cézanne married a woman of Aix, plain and not very intelligent, but a good wife to him, never interfering with his painting and sitting like Patience on a monument when he needed a human model. During the Franco-Prussian War, he sidestepped military service and went on painting; and when the impressionists, headed by Renoir and Pissarro, held their first exhibition in 1874, he was one of them, and the most vilified of the lot. With the meanness for which the French critics have long been notorious—when not bought outright—the scribes tore Cézanne limb from limb: he was a clodhopper and an ignoramus, a Zulu with a brush, a butcher who made designs, as depraved children did, by squeezing flies between folds of paper. But for the fighting good will of Zola, with whom he had passed his boyhood in Aix, and a few enlightened artists, he could never have taken the critical onslaught. Having no need to sell his paintings, and despising Paris with peasant antipathies, he spent more and more time in the South and after an exhibition, in 1895, which was viciously manhandled, he retired permanently to his estate in Provence, "sick of the whole damned art racket," he swore.

In the ten years left to him, he carried his easel into the open air, growing more solitary and irascible with time, destroying canvases, throwing them out of his studio windows and abandoning them in the field or giving them to his son as plans for jigsaw puzzles. At the opening of the century, the *cognoscenti* began to discover the value of his efforts, and one slick dealer, Vollard, journeyed to the South to buy up everything in sight. The peasants, hearing that an old fool from Paris was actually paying hard money for the pictures of the local fool, dug up scores of canvases they had retrieved from the fields. And the old master of Aix was filled with joy. At last, he was making a stir in the world! But it was too late to do him any good, and in 1906, while painting in the rain, he caught a fever that struck him down.

After his death, the fame of the groping hermit of Aix steadily rose, and he became the most influential of modern painters; in fact the one and only, and the legitimate father of modernism in art. But the vituperative provincial would gyre and gimble in his grave if he could behold the crimes committed in his name. "I am only a helpless pioneer on a lonely road," he complained; but the road was the right one, and though his paintings, for the most part, are plainly the results of a trial-

and-error method, they were put together by one who understood the great qualities of the old masters and who had his own ideas for the restoration of art to a position of respect and eminence.

Cézanne was on the road leading to the heights, a tragic figure, helpless without models and helpless in their presence, self-torturing, ineffably painstaking and never satisfied. Recognizing the shallowness of the painting of his own time, both the old academic stuff and the departures of the impressionists with whom he was allied because of his interest in color, he aspired, from the depths of his soul, to create pictures as solid and durable as the museum masterpieces; pictures that would move and ennoble people, but fresh and clean and modern, not antiquities or dark things for specialists. He wanted to make pictures that were real and true; to build up a rich, full world in three dimensions wherein one might receive experiences comparable in force to those of our practical life.

Unfortunately, he was not a Rubens or a Leonardo. He was inordinately timid and pathetically loaded down with temperamental baggage. He had an erotic passion for the nude, a lifelong desire to pose a naked woman on the banks of the river near his estate in the South, but he never did. He was afraid. "All women are cats and damned calculating," he said. "And they might get their hooks into me." In consequence, his paintings of the nude are far from satisfactory, having been made from reproductions of the old-timers, or from his memory of the decrepit showgirls of the art schools of Paris. His renderings of the uncovered female are not likely to cudgel the curiosity of modern boys and girls who go to the beaches or look at pictorial magazines. His women are crude distortions, distinguishable from his men only by their enlarged hindquarters.

Incapable of commanding what he desired most, Cézanne withdrew into the world of landscapes and into the kingdom of vegetables. Before the withdrawal, he paid his respects to portraiture, but for the life of him, could find only a few sitters immobile enough to face the ordeal of posing. There was his homely wife, of course, who sat by the hour, by the day, by the week, as the bearded painter examined the light on each plane of her peasant face and translated it into singing colors. Madame Cézanne, in the best of the portraits, resembles a beautifully tinted mask on a solid neck attached to a body of cement. His portrait of a friendly critic, M. Geffroy—his only friendly critic —required 90 sittings; and that of Vollard, the dealer who gobbled up his paintings, 115 sittings, after which the painter remarked, "The front of the shirt is not bad." His best portrait is that of himself, a face he knew by heart after thousands of studies, and in painting it, he showed us what he might have achieved with other faces if the owners had been willing to sit like wooden images for years and years; and to submit to his agonizing process of applying paint, touch by touch, tone by tone, color by color.

When he addressed himself to landscape, Cézanne relied on the natural pattern of the country he had been intimate with from birth, adhering as closely to the geological formations as he did to the features of living models whom he persuaded to pose for him in his studio. His landscapes are landmarks in the painting of nature, but his greatest contribution to art is to be found in his still life. Here his spirit was emancipated—fruits and flowers opened their hearts to him, and he cast his eyes upon them in the spirit of a lover doting on his first mistress. No bored females who hated his integrity; no landscapes to be mapped and charted, but fruits and flowers on a blue tablecloth, welcoming his brush until the final stages of decomposition.

If Cézanne's pictures of men and women leave his models in a state of paralysis, and his landscapes seem primordial and volcanic, his still lifes are the works of a master. His compositions of fruits and vegetables are more dramatic than the human beings of most artists; they have the weight, the nobility and the style of immortal forms—the sterling virtues of nuggets of gold which cannot be effaced by time or attrition. No other painter ever brought to a red apple, or an orange on a blue cloth, a conviction so heated or an observation so protracted. Cézanne found his humanity, his "little piece of gold," he called it, in still life, and he reserved for flowers and fruits his strongest impulses to the making of new and living things. Since his death, thousands upon thousands of artists have tried to transfer their passions to still life, but their efforts, in comparison, are imitative and unnecessary.

To the general public, Cézanne today, more than forty years after his death, is still something of an enigma—garrulously extolled in many camps, hated in others, and among conventional painters unhesitatingly regarded as a bungler and a sham promoted by misfits and the aggressive elements of modernism. I find that most observant people, at least those not too timid to speak their minds, find his still lifes stunning and dramatic; his landscapes —or a few of them—convincing and beautiful in color, though unfinished; and his portraits and nudes simply unintelligible. This appraisal of the old hermit of Aix is about as it should be, since the man's great reputation is based, for the most part, upon his technical innovations and experiments, and upon the invigorating effect he had on art when it was bogged down by flashy salon performances and the charming, though shallow efforts, of impressionists who sat in the open air and copied the vibrating tones of natural light.

Of Cézanne's aims there can be no dispute: they were identical with the aims of the old masters. Awkward and incomplete in paint, he was capable at times of verbal precision, as, for example, when he said that he strove to make out of impressionism something as solid and durable as the great paintings of the museums. But in his strivings, he grappled with one of the most complicated techniques ever chosen by a painter for his own headaches. He had a wonderful color sense, and tried to devise a method whereby he could construct figures and objects of monumental solidity yet as bright in color as the works of the impressionists. He did not succeed, and applying paint in small segments and patches, could only reveal the planes and surfaces of things when he intended to present the masses. That is why his paintings look unfinished.

There is no need, in this book, to go into the hundred and one cults which owe their existence to Cézanne's pioneering efforts. It will be enough to point out that the painters of the modern school of Paris, with Picasso as leader, have evolved out of Cézanne's studies a brand of painting known as abstract, or non-representative, or non-objective. That means, in brief, they enlarged upon the planes of his pictures and extended them, with the result that the subject and all natural appearances were destroyed, and nothing was left but some splinters and cubes.

GEORGE BELLOWS was the most popular painter of his time and an American to the core without being a Babbitt or a chauvinist. He was a natural, to borrow a word coined by a sports writer in referring to the prodigious talents of another good American, Dizzy Dean, and he fell into the pattern of our folkways as unceremoniously as a red Indian rode bareback over the prairies. He came into the art of painting as Mark Twain came into the art of writing, and more than any other American, he made painting a reputable occupation. I mean that he rescued it from the idlers, pretenders and esthetes who went abroad for their ideas and their culture and who returned to look upon their countrymen as vulgarians.

Bellows never went to Europe—not that he was against it, for he was generous and open-minded, but he was too busy with his own people, and too vigorously absorbed in native subject matter to take a holiday in foreign lands. Europe would not have helped him, and it might have hampered him —there is no way of telling—but it was probably for the best that he did not expose his extraordinarily receptive personality to the arty contagions of the Continent. Willing to try anything once, he was sometimes misled by specious nostrums for the creation of pictures, but his native intelligence always restored him to his proper habits.

Appropriately enough, Bellows came from the heart of America—the Middle West—but he did not boast immoderately about it. He was born in Columbus, Ohio, in 1882, the descendant of a long line of Englishmen, the first of whom, Benjamin Bellows, migrated to the Colonies in 1632. His ancestors were seafaring men who chased whales in the North Atlantic and settled in Vermont before joining the exodus to the Ohio valleys. After the usual preparation at high school, he entered Ohio State University, a mass-production, educational plant—and a good one—where he is still remembered for his skill in baseball. He was, I have been privately informed, a major league prospect who played the national game professionally during the summer months, a practice not frowned upon in those carefree days. His drawing developed along with his skill in sports and he was, as an undergraduate, a semiprofessional artist, or cartoonist, for a local newspaper.

Bellows was by temperament an artist, and in his senior year waved farewell to Ohio State and moved to New York to study painting. By good luck, he came under the inspiring guidance of Robert Henri, and his progress was record-breaking. At twenty-seven, he was made an associate of the National Academy, the youngest man to win that distinction, and in the same year, the Metropolitan Museum bought one of his pictures, a purchase which made him the youngest artist, but one, to be recognized by the Museum.

In 1910, he married Emma Louise Story, and bought a house on East Nineteenth Street, the Bellows house which has become a shrine, if shrines are possible in New York. Here he received friends from all stations—artists, writers, athletes, bankers—and here his daughters, Anne and Jean, the models for many pictures, passed their childhood; and here he rose swiftly to a position of nationwide acclaim. Once secure, he worked steadily in oils, lithography and illustration, lending his support to all sorts of social and humanitarian causes, and taking an honest stand in behalf of the underdog. In 1925, hardly in his prime, an attack of appendicitis put an end to his career, and American art suffered a calamity. The memorial exhibition of his work held in the Metropolitan shortly after his death surpassed the Museum's records for attendance, and I remember how reverently old and young, art students and journalists, trooped before the canvases filling the high walls. For Bellows was a man among men, a living artist and an exponent of his own people, and without cheapening his standards, produced pictures which were enjoyed and loved by millions.

Famous Artists and Their Models

It was in character that Bellows, like Stephen Crane, should have been a baseball player, since both were artists in the robust sense of the word, drawing upon the abounding vitality of everyday life for their materials. While many painters stewed and fretted over their subjects and traveled here and there for seemly material, Bellows, in a walk around the block, would discover enough material to last him for months. He took a natural, not a forced interest in his subjects, and the panorama of American life, from the prize ring to the revival meetings of Billy Sunday, from the pastoral scenes of Woodstock to the execution of Nurse Cavell, invoked his prodigal energies as the life of Flanders, in the old days, inflamed the imagination of Rubens.

The art of George Bellows began at home. His family came first: his wife in all her beauty and his daughters from year to year—among the best portraits in American painting. Going out from his doorstep, he portrayed the world—men and women of note and children on the sandlots—all with warmth, speed and sympathy but without flattery or satire. His social consciousness developed—but he never sold his talents to the propagandists—and he made drawings for liberal magazines, with John Sloan and Glackens; drawings of the lowly and unfortunate. He was one of the first to practice lithography to any extent in America and at times, forced to contain his restlessness, he made prints which are preferred by many of his devotees to his larger works in oil. The dead-end kids swimming in the ferry slips were his models, and his aged mother, and the polo players in the fashionable meadows of Long Island, and some cross-eyed urchin he had collared in a vacant lot.

Occasionally, being a gullible American, he succumbed to patent theories such as the Hambidge scheme of dynamic symmetry, a method of making pictures by abstract logic; and the Maratta color scales, which were intended to spare the artist the necessity of mixing his own tones—but these short-cuts to creation did not seriously affect his production. The gaudy, riotous, native scene always corrected his mistakes and he went on his merry way, tempted by the dynamic elements of our country, and by the picturesque, and leaving us, at his early death, not only a legacy of pictures, but an example for the troubled boys and girls of today to take to heart, when they set out to study painting.

In the year before his death, I had a long discussion with Bellows on a subject which, at that particular moment, was uppermost in the minds of American artists. The subject was the value of European training in the development of American talent, and since most of our young students went to Paris to learn how to paint, those who favored an interlude on the Continent, before settling down to a professional career, were having the best of the argument. Bellows, as I have said, championed a small but increasing number of artists who contended that a residence abroad was injurious in most cases.

"Of course I'd like to go to Paris," he said, "but only to have some fun. But the idea that it is really essential for our youngsters to live in the Latin Quarter is an old superstition fostered by the French for economic reasons. Now mind you, I have nothing against European art. As a matter of fact, I've been greatly influenced by it—perhaps too much so—and men like Hals and Manet have helped me find myself. And there was a time, no doubt—before our museums were stocked with Old World masterpieces—when a painter had to visit the galleries of Europe in order to study the rulers of the craft.

"It is different today, and when I want to look at the old painters, I take a day off and visit the Metropolitan Museum. In this way I do not lose the firsthand contacts with my models and subjects. I find that most of our students, after living abroad for any length of time, return to America with a fixed set of painting habits that eventually ruins them, and with the mischievous notion that America is no place for anyone with creative aspirations. This, in my opinion, is nonsense. But I don't bother too much about it. I have too much to do, and like Daumier, I have a public."

ABOUT twenty years ago, when American artists
were bending low before European models,
and trying their best to make themselves over into
French Bohemians, a counter-movement gathered
momentum in this country. The leaders of the
movement were five men whose work not only
lifted them into national prominence but put an
end, for the time being, to our provincial servility.
The men were Charles Burchfield, Thomas Hart
Benton, Grant Wood, John Steuart Curry, and
Reginald Marsh—bold and independent Americans
who took art into the open air, away from the
jurisdiction of esthetes and political fanatics, and
within the reach of the people. Two of them are
gone now, Wood and Curry, but the remaining
three are still producing the most original pictures
of our time.

The pioneer in the revolt against European imi-
tation was Charles Burchfield, a tailor's son born in
Ohio, in 1893. Burchfield is one of those grim,
gifted, self-sufficient Americans who take nothing
for granted, a Middle Westerner with the melan-
choly, sharp-seeing interest in hard facts which

characterizes the novelists of the central valleys. He was brought up in a rustic background; in drab, down-at-the-heels towns and monotonous farm lands that no one loved. But the life of the midlands made a profound impression on him, as he wandered at random observing the habits of men and women, the wretched architecture, the long freight trains, the fields and forlorn vistas of unoccupied earth, the farmers and their sad-faced wives, and the social life of the shabby settlements.

In his youth, Burchfield attended an art school in Cleveland, and in his late twenties exhibited in New York a collection of water colors of astonishing originality. This young man brought painting down to earth. He painted the country that was in his blood—the Midwestern environment that had matured his conception of America, and he did not look at his birthright through the tinted glasses of French impressionism. His models were scenes and subjects that were supposed to be intrinsically ugly; but he was truthful and his experiences had taught him that life was seldom charming and never classical. Beneath the loneliness and monotony of the country, he discovered nobility of effort and a naked, haunting grandeur.

He painted villages in winter, the coming of spring, the summer harvests and fall ploughing; he studied the countryside as another artist would study human anatomy, drawing and painting the rows of false-front stores straggling on one side of the highway, farmers in Model-T Fords, and the local architecture from the dilapidated cottages by the tracks to the jigsaw Gothic of the quality folks. Of late years, Burchfield has been living in the country near Buffalo, New York, and his work has steadily increased in richness and poetry. He has extracted from American life an art that may justly be called his own, and to pronounce him one of the best of living painters is only a half-tribute.

The most prominent, vigorous and versatile of our painters is Thomas Hart Benton, born in Missouri, in 1889, the grand-nephew of the old Missouri Senator and the son of a Congressman and criminal lawyer. The backwoods country of his boyhood was not unlike that of Huckleberry Finn, but he had the advantage of winters in Washington and extensive traveling. At nineteen, he went to Paris, as most students did, and after five years in the art colony on the Left Bank, returned home a dismal misfit. He lived in New York for a number of years, but it was not until he settled in the country of his boyhood and thoroughly Americanized himself that he found the true nature of his abilities.

For a score of years, Benton has made annual excursions into the hinterlands and distant reaches of the United States. With a knapsack of drawing materials on his back, he has journeyed from the industrial centers to the mountain nooks and backwoods. He understands people high and low, and people like him, put him up for the night, swap yarns with him, and pose for him. In the course of his wanderings he has amassed a library of notes and drawings: cowboys, mountaineers, college professors, cotton pickers, politicians, mill hands, Indians, rustic fiddlers, harvest hands, poets and preachers—every one drawn from life and from models beyond the endurance, not to say the tastes, of other modern painters. Eventually, these studies find their way into his finished canvases in oil and tempera.

Benton has executed four large murals of outstanding significance in contemporary painting, two in New York, one in Indiana, and one in Missouri, and all storm centers of controversy The reason for the uproar is that he has flouted the conventions of wall painting—the sylvan cuties pursued by satyrs, or dumb goddesses with G-strings of cheesecloth. He has painted actual scenes and living characters—in the Missouri mural, the James boys and Boss Pendergast—scenes of crime and violence, agrarian occupations, industrial activities, night life in cities; and he has painted them with a full-bodied, dynamic style unknown to art since the days of Dutch genre. Benton makes his home in Kansas City, and though his aggressiveness has slackened a little, his energy and his interest in the behavior of his people seem to expand with age.

Another Middle Westerner was John Steuart Curry, a Kansas product born on a farm in 1897, and an extremely sensitive artist who came by his materials naturally. From the hard grind of his daily life, he gained his knowledge of crops and cattle, and developed at an early age his affection for all kinds of animal life. He lived in a country of sudden and unpredictable changes of weather, and every day of his life heard talk about the weather and the destructive forces of nature. He observed the terrors and apprehensions of farmers, and in happier vein, the rejoicing when the spring rains fell, and the grain ripened, and the wheat and corn were safely stored. As a boy, Curry attempted to depict the intimate business of farm life; as a mature artist he painted the same things and won great renown, producing in a few years the most memorable genre painting in our annals. The subjects were important to him, and his interpretation of them is important to a clear understanding of our countrymen.

In all his works—murals, lithographs, book illustrations, storms, and animals—Curry worked from realities, from models directly perceived and studied; but in the process of construction leading to the finished pictures, there entered into his imagination a love for his subjects, with its feelings and memories, and he became a poet, the most poetic of latter-day American artists. His landscape, *The Line Storm*, is a masterpiece in which the earth is transformed into a terrifying personality; and in his *Wisconsin Landscape* he brings out

the majesty and opulence of land beautifully cultivated. Before his untimely death in 1946, he lived
in Madison as artist-in-residence to the University
of Wisconsin, a post he had occupied for a term
of years.

When Grant Wood died, in 1942, in his fiftieth
year, he was almost a national institution, if that
may be said of any painter, and no one has come
along to take his place. He was born in Iowa, lived
his whole life in Iowa—save a couple of wild-goose
chases to Europe—and won his recognition in the
Middle West, without promotion from New York,
in itself an achievement. Born in poverty, he was
also born with a genius for the arts and crafts, and
performed almost every kind of manual toil from
masonry to metalwork. He was an accomplished
painter at fifteen; a country school teacher, and a
powerful influence in regional art, which, to him,
meant simply the painting of the subjects one grew
up with and understood; and during his last years,
head of the art department of the University of
Iowa to which he gave generously of his unique
talents.

Before he found himself, Wood painted nice
impressionist landscapes, skilfully executed canvases in which Iowa farm lands resembled the
countryside of France; but his solid base in the
crafts and his common sense eventually triumphed,
and in his comparatively short life he produced
portraits ranking with the best done in America,

and some masterly pieces of designing like the *Dinner for Threshers*. His sister and a local dentist acted as models for his *American Gothic*, one of the most deservedly popular pictures in American art, and an example of his incisive characterization rendered with craftsmanship of the highest order. His celebrated *Woman with Plants* is a portrait of his mother who stood by him and struggled with him in his battle for recognition.

Among the younger artists who have come forward since World War I, Reginald Marsh stands apart as the offspring of the city, a painter concerned exclusively with the urban scene. After his schooling at Lawrenceville and Yale, he settled in New York where, in a short time, he became conspicuous for his studies of the humbler aspects of metropolitan life. Many artists have portrayed New York, and many have been swayed by its magnitude and vitality; but none, to my knowledge, has approached it with the affection of Marsh. This man really loves the town, particularly the grand vulgarity and incomparable glamor of the life in Fourteenth Street, and lives in an apartment in the very heart of his chosen quarter.

One of the most intelligent artists now functioning, Marsh has never been trapped by the shallow theories and show-off art of our day. Of even temperament and with no disposition to turn his pictures into propaganda, he is an observer of life in the best sense, as Hogarth was, and Daumier.

The smart circles of society do not interest him; well-bred people bore him and he cannot paint them with any degree of success. But the girls of Coney Island and the burlesque houses inspire him, and he accepts the voluptuous queens of Fourteenth Street with their gaudy sensuality as affectionately as Rubens accepted the strapping Flemish girls, or Renoir the healthy wenches of France. He is an artist of power, one of the best of living draftsmen, with a sensual tenderness in his style and a wise appreciation of exposed flesh. Some of his recent studies of young girls—large studies in Chinese ink made from portrait sketches —have attained a quality that can only be called classical.

Despite his contention that most painters have too many irons in the fire and dissipate their energies, and that he is happy to confine himself to a few subjects, Marsh took time from his favorite models to decorate, in fresco, the Customs House in New York with monumental representations of ocean liners and the congestions of landings and departures—one of the best of twentieth-century murals.

IN these days of printing difficulties at home, and the scarcity of European importations, the problem of illustrating a book on art with the best pictures obtainable is an author's headache. I must express my special indebtedness to Herman J. Wechsler, of the F.A.R. Gallery, New York, for his generous assistance in solving this problem.

I must also thank the following galleries and publishers of fine prints for permission to use their prints and original paintings in making the plates for this book:

ERICH S. HERRMANN, representing Braun & Co. of Paris, and The Medici Society of London, for the following:
1. *Head of Christ*, Leonardo da Vinci 2. *Mary, Jesus, St. Elizabeth and St. John*, Leonardo da Vinci 3. *Mary, Jesus and St. Anne*, Leonardo da Vinci 6. *Toilet of Venus*, Titian 7. *Man with a Glove*, Titian 8. *Portrait of Richard Southwell*, Holbein 11. *Portrait of a Woman*, Rubens 13. *Rembrandt and Wife*, Rembrandt 14. *Maja Vestida*, Goya 15. *Maja Desnuda*, Goya 16. *Infanta*, Velasquez 22. *Blue Corn*, Van Gogh 26. *The Mill at Pontoise*, Cézanne. Inside front cover: *Vincent's House at Arles*, Van Gogh.

DAVID ASHLEY, INC., representing Roberto Hoesch of Milan, for the following:
4. *Adam (Detail from The Creation)*, Michelangelo
5. *Jeremiah*, Michelangelo 25. *Apples and Primroses (Detail)*, Cézanne (Collection of Mr. and Mrs. Sam A. Lewisohn)

SIMON AND SCHUSTER, INC., New York, for the following:
9. *Artist and His First Wife*, Rubens 10. *Judgment of Paris (Detail)*, Rubens 21. *Le Déjeuner sur l'Herbe*, Manet

Acknowledgments

THE NATIONAL GALLERY OF ART, Washington, D. C., for the following:

18. *Keelmen Heaving in Coals by Moonlight, Turner* (Widener Collection)   27. *Both Members of This Club, Bellows* (Gift of Chester Dale). Inside back cover: *Edward VI as Prince of Wales, Holbein* (Mellon Collection)

THE MORGAN LIBRARY, New York, for the following:

19. *The Morning Stars Sang Together, Blake*

THE MUSEUM OF MODERN ART, New York, for the following:

23. *La Goulue, Toulouse-Lautrec* (Collection of Dr. and Mrs. David Levy)

ANTON SCHUTZ, of the New York Graphic Society, for the following:

27. *Both Members of This Club, Bellows*   28. *American Gothic, Wood*   32. *Promenade, Burchfield.* Inside back cover: *Edward VI as Prince of Wales, Holbein*

THE ART INSTITUTE OF CHICAGO, for the following:
28. *American Gothic, Wood*

ASSOCIATED AMERICAN ARTISTS GALLERIES, New York, for the following:
28. *American Gothic, Wood*   30. *The Music Lesson, Benton*

A. ROTHMANN, FINE ARTS, INC., representing Anton Schroll of Vienna (Color Prints), for the following:

Front cover: *Toilette of Venus, Rubens.* Back cover: *The Officer's Wife, Rembrandt*

Right →

HANS HOLBEIN: *Edward VI as Prince of Wales*